AF244104

MEDITATION TIME
Know Yourself and the World Around You

Laurent Grenier

PHILOSOPHICAL ESSAY

NardisPress

CIP data on file at the Library
and Archives Canada
ISBN 978-0-9737200-1-3

BY THE SAME AUTHOR

A Reason for Living
(autobiographical and philosophical essay)
NardisPress, October 2004

CONTENTS

Foreword

The title of this philosophical essay, much like the first chapter, bears the stamp of a well-known maxim by the Greek philosopher Socrates, whose call for self-knowledge was also an invitation to know the outside world. Furthermore, it was the prerequisite for a good life, which he regarded as a practical goal of utmost importance that destined everyone to be philosophers, often informally and without the scholarly credentials of academics.

I can certainly identify with that, especially since my philosophical journey was prompted in my teens when my life took a turn for the worst and left me in limbo, between the survival instinct and the hunger for meaning. I had broken my neck in a diving accident and lost in a fateful second the physical abilities I had enjoyed until then, thinking that I was by nature entitled to them for the rest of my days. I was strong, athletic, seemingly indestructible, though susceptible to minor ailments. And yet, against all expectations, there I was, largely paralyzed from the neck down.

How could I be both alive and physically dead in a manner of speaking, incapable of pursuing the very things that mattered most to me, sporty things among others that I lived and loved with the comforting belief that my future would bring into blossom the many promises that my present was budding with? In short, to my mind, paralysis involved a painful contradiction that made no sense whatever. A prevailing feeling of absurdity washed over me like a wave of formidable strength that threatened to drown me. I was gasping for air, for an answer to the existential question, "why live, and how?"

This question changed me through and through, from a brawny and outdoorsy teen to a broody young man who was admitted—for lack of a better, manageable option, after months in a hospital—to a long-term care facility that was to be my new home: a dreary, antiquated institution, like a relic of the Victorian age where mostly decrepit and senile old folks were relegated as the last indignity before their passing. An odd collective way of thanking these folks for decades of service as contributing citizens!

Today, my physical condition is roughly the same, with the exigencies of old age thrown into the mix, but fortunately my circumstances have otherwise improved. Blessed daily by the vital assistance of capable and gracious caregivers, I live in an apartment adapted to my special needs. Nearly a half century has passed, which I have spent largely indoors, like a meditative and studious monk, steeped in mindful attention to my present and the rich culture of my time, comprising every branch of human knowledge. Gratefully indebted to this cultural heritage, I now reap the benefits of meaningful insights that are conducive to serenity and contentment. I gleaned them along the way with an increasingly cheerful disposition.

I do not claim to be a professional philosopher, that is, a bona fide academic, born of a university, with a frameable doctorate to display on a wall. My insights are simply the product of my determination to escape a wretched prison of my own design, as I failed to see the light that remained in the darkness beyond the horizon of my ignorance. The purpose of this book is to share with you, dear reader, these salutary insights—many of which implicitly or explicitly echo those of prominent thinkers of the past—in the hope of helping you discover your own truth and experience such joy and inner peace as the ones that have so gloriously transfigured my life. As a mere human, this is the closest I came to rising from the dead and spreading the good word. Not the kind of message that demands allegiance to divine authority, but one that encourages people to think for themselves toward a wholesome philosophy of life that is at best universal, yet personal and transformative in the most enterprising and loving way that is humanly possible.

Before we go any further, let me shed light on the way of this book, whose structural and thematic profile is loose and disparate—reminiscent of an English garden, combining a poetic form of human order with the spontaneous vagaries of natural growth, as opposed to a garden *à la française,* sporting a manicured appearance of rational perfection. This may be disconcerting to some readers, perhaps expecting a more linear and convergent mode of exposition, with an engaging start, a gradual and logical development, and a satisfying end. Indeed, upon glancing at the contents or riffling through my book to get an idea of what lies ahead, you may scratch your head over my various chapters whose arrangement or inclusion—given my initial focus on the meaning of life and the art of living—may seem at times questionable.

The truth is, my book appears untidy and incomplete because it is, despite my best effort to approach the mystery of existence in a factual, coherent, and luminous fashion. I see no point to a system of thought whose pretense of tidiness and completeness amounts in the end to a pure illusion. Any serious answer to the existential question "why live, and how" is inevitably destined to be variegated and unfinished, because it deals with an organic subject presenting an abundance of contrasting and related aspects that constitute a complex and dynamic whole, impossible to exhaust by force of understanding, be it scientific or philosophical.

Take for example self-awareness. Like the lobby of a mansion that opens onto a room, which opens onto another room and so on and so forth, it leads successively to a vast range of issues like that of human nature and empirical knowledge, or that of divine principle and universal determinism, together with a host of intimately connected others that are also extremely diverse.

Consequently, I urge you to regard this book as an opportunity to embark on a thinking adventure, a kind of treasure hunt whose success depends on your willingness to actively participate. My modest contribution to this adventure consists of the salutary insights I mentioned earlier. They are clues that are strewn along the way to help you navigate the difficult terrain of existence. At times you will choose to follow these clues; at other times you will challenge them on the basis of contrary intuitions. Whatever works to bring you ever closer to the coveted treasure is the right course. What exactly is this treasure? It is a eureka moment thanks to which the world makes sense to you and life is worth the struggle.

I dedicate this book to Pierre Demers,
my brother in spirit
who saved me from drowning in 1974
and is alas now deceased,
and to Mona,
daughter of my late, beloved friend,
Halim Harb

I also want to affectionately thank
my blood brother Pierre Grenier
for his extremely bright
and learned presence in my life
that has always proven very stimulating

Lastly, I want to extend my gratitude
to the editor James Dryden who,
together with Nejc Vidic
and my lifelong friend Claude Soucie,
perused my manuscript
and made valuable observations

Please be advised that on a few occasions
in this essay I have used the term
"entropy"—meaning the tendency of
closed systems to evolve toward
thermodynamic equilibrium—in
reference to this equilibrium as the
end product of this tendency

Self-Awareness

"The only sure path of self-discovery is our own existence as an object of meditative observation."

Let us start with Socrates' philosophical imperative: Know yourself! This is great advice, as any effort to lead a fulfilling life without first striving to achieve self-awareness is like building a house before learning the fundamentals of the construction trade. Such a building endeavor could never amount to anything that we would feel inspired to call home.

How do we go about knowing ourselves? The answer lies in paying attention to the truth of our nature as we experience it daily. That said, this attention has a prerequisite: We must at least be willing, if not raring, to face the truth; and that in itself is a daunting challenge. Indeed, truth is often painfully unsettling, and we humans have an inborn tendency to evade suffering by way of diversion and mindlessness or denial and fancifulness, which are impediments to truth. Yet, daunting as it is, this challenge calls for a stoic act of lucidity where we bring to the forefront of our consciousness the very aspects of our lives that we find the most difficult to cope with.

This new demand—exhorting us to face squarely and bravely our unpleasant truths—should not be left at that. We have both the freedom and the power, and therefore the duty to help ourselves rise to the challenge. To this effect, we ought to cultivate our ability to cope insofar as it is the necessary condition for our ability to learn. As mentioned earlier, the latter is indispensable to the process of self-discovery for the purpose of a wise and happy life.

The thing is, we are sentient beings who are extremely vulnerable at the psychological level, and our so-called rational nature is greatly overstated. What we cannot process psychologically, for lack of accepting it, we cannot process rationally, with the result that we fail to acknowledge the truth and instead indulge in wishful thinking. Again, allow me to emphasize the fact that such a misguided way is in total contradiction with the act of turning a negative situation into a positive one through self-awareness and self-realization.

Fortunately, our weaknesses are paired with strengths that can proudly offset them. Among those strengths is our innate adaptability. While it usually exceeds by a wide margin our assumptions about it or is grossly underestimated, it can be developed by degrees as we overcome various hardships thanks to some resourceful adjustments.

In the meantime, we may feel somewhat emboldened by the example of others who have proven remarkably adaptable, or capable of coping with significant upsets. But this courage by proxy is always subject to doubt and can waver. Others are not us, even though they may share with us some common traits and experiences. We can always question the relevance of their example as far as we are concerned. It follows that faith in our human faculties, physical or mental, is most invigorating if derived from an intimate knowledge of these faculties when we successfully exercise them.

A similar statement can be made regarding our knowledge of human nature in general. So long as it is acquired through lessons alone, imparted to us by enlightened others, it feels abstract and hollow, hardly real, largely uncertain. It may broaden the horizon of our curiosity, beyond the scope of our current empirical knowledge, and make us less complacent or arrogant, in a word more humble. As such it can be useful. However, the only sure path of self-discovery is our own existence as an object of meditative observation. This is especially true with respect to our unique individuality, which is completely outside the purview of education. The latter deals solely in generalities and hence has no predictive value for our individual characteristics.

In conclusion, the better we know ourselves as individuals, namely our unique blend of abilities and limitations, of needs and desires, and responsibilities, the more we are likely to make the right choices to achieve well-being and peace of mind. Of course this likelihood does not exclude the risk of mistakes or failures, which relate to the chronic imperfection of our knowledge: a lifelong work in progress that merely stops at death. But if we are fortunate enough to survive these mistakes or failures, we can learn from them and increase our chances of succeeding proudly and joyfully in the future.

Summary of Self-Awareness:

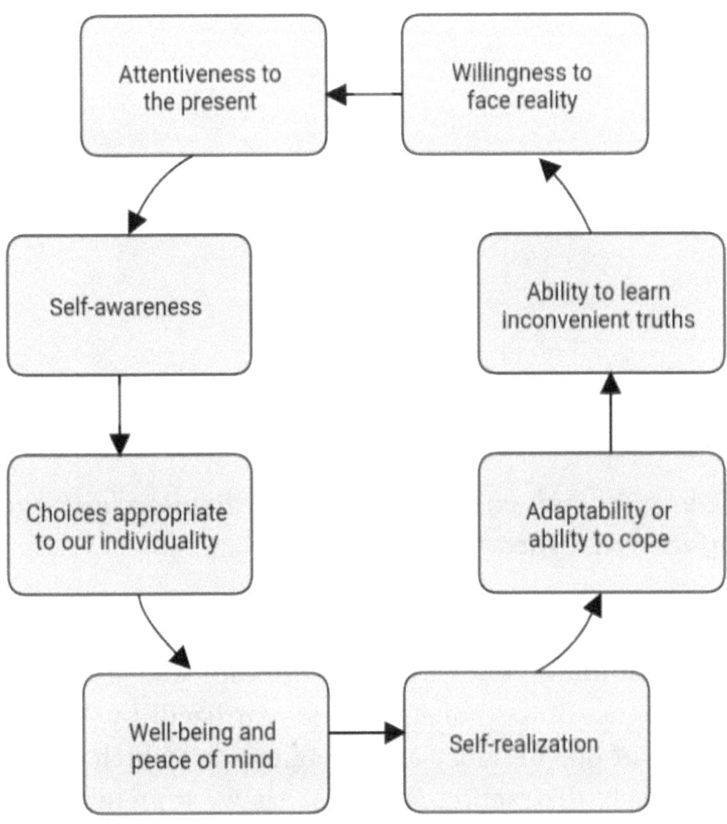
Attentiveness to the present
Willingness to face reality
Self-awareness
Ability to learn inconvenient truths
Choices appropriate to our individuality
Adaptability or ability to cope
Well-being and peace of mind
Self-realization

Here and Now

"The so-called easy way out is always chock-full of unforeseen difficulties."

While the present is a window of experience that affords us an intimate view of our nature and that of the world around us, it is constantly jeopardized by the inner chatter of our memory and imagination, which can prove immensely distracting. The past, as we remember it, and the future, as we plan, wish, or fear it, are therefore in direct competition with the present, as we live it.

And the risk of distraction doesn't stop there. Our attention to the present can be indiscriminately divided between a host of things ranging from the most important to the most insignificant. The worst among us are scatterbrains, prone to mishaps because of their lack of mental discipline. They do too many things at once in a disconnected, careless fashion.

Human consciousness, however, is a limited resource that can be overwhelmed with an excess of input from different sources. It demands a clear sense of priority and focus, lest it should lapse into a jumbled heap of information that we are unable to effectively process, leaving us dazed and confused.

This is as tall an order as it is pressing. Discipline, indeed, doesn't come to us spontaneously. It proceeds from an informed and mature decision to resist humoring the child within us whose unruly playfulness has its time and place but must also be tamed if we care to grow beyond the stage of mindless infantilism. Likewise, though we share with monkeys the same origin, we are designed to overtake them on the evolutionary road and ideally become exemplars of wisdom, rectitude, kindness, and proficiency.

Again, we must be wary of the pitfalls along the way that can hold us back. They are all the more treacherous as we naturally gravitate toward them, like deer attracted by the headlights of cars that barrel at night along country roads. If only they knew better than to follow their instincts when their instincts—aimed in principle at their preservation—ironically lead to their tragic demise.

We, on the other hand, should have enough sense to prevent our minds from wandering without restraint. Such foolishness may be our natural inclination, a path of least resistance that appeals to the lazy demon lurking inside us, but the so-called easy way out is always chock-full of unforeseen difficulties. Our humanity cannot thrive in a hectic existence of scattered actions that move jointly with a whirling mass of blurry feelings and fuzzy thoughts. And what could be more painful than seeing in the mirror an old reflection of ourselves, with only wrinkles and aches to testify for the passage of time, as we stand void of any worthy achievement? What could be harder to deal with than this rude awakening when we no longer have the luxury of youth to redeem ourselves, and death awaits us contemptuously?

Before closing, allow me to expand on one insidious pitfall that takes the form of a strength but acts like a weakness. It does so to the extent that it compounds the risk of distraction—which is also a risk of destruction as regards our prospect of fulfillment—in all spheres of human activity. As we know, there can be no fulfillment without mindfulness.

We are reputedly creatures of habit, and that increasingly as we age. We learn to prefer caution to temerity and replace the itch for adventure with a taste for comfort. At home, at work, and elsewhere, we readily settle into familiar ways of getting things done, namely routines. And the greater the familiarity, the more we are likely to let our minds drift while we go on autopilot in the thoughtless manner of an automaton. As a result, our sense of purpose and accomplishment is severely dulled, and our robotic life seems more and more like a pointless exercise. Depression sets in.

Yet, instead of resorting to further escapism to bury our low spirits, we would be well advised to shake things up by changing for the better certain mediocre habits that we have tolerated until now, much to our shame, but also and mostly to snap out of our zombie ways. Only then can we see a silver lining beyond our cloudy past, as we thoughtfully reinvest our every action with meaning and value, and finally rediscover the joy of living.

Summary of Here and Now:

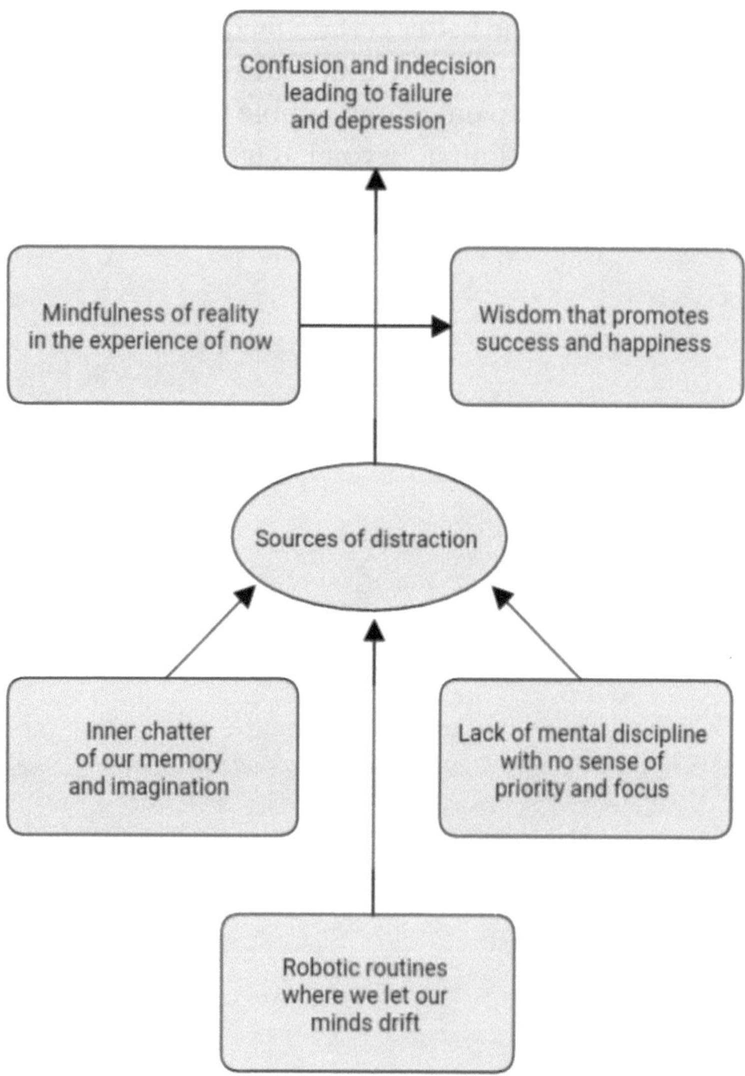

Self-Realization

"We may consider our habits satisfying, but we should never forget that our nature includes an inborn capacity for adaptation."

From the moment we are conceived until we breathe our last, we interact with our environment: at first, the intrauterine world of our mother, herself interacting with the world around her, then directly this outside world. Whatever our stage of growth or maturity, this environment represents a unique set of challenges and opportunities that compels us to seek viable, adaptive answers that shape our way of being.

We can therefore distinguish between our genetic makeup, which comprises an unfathomable array of developmental possibilities, and our individual experience, in the relatively narrow context of our interaction with our existing circumstances where we realize but a fraction of our human potential. Let us name the former "our primary self" and the latter "our secondary self."

Our primary self is static and largely undifferentiated within the confines of basic humanness, whereas our secondary self is highly differentiated and fluid or rigid depending on whether or not we are open to changing our way of being. This openness may be necessary when our situation is turned upside down and renders some of our habits impossible or impractical; or it may be optional, absent any external pressure, leaving us free to keep our habits or change them for the sake of novelty.

At any given time, our self-awareness bears on our secondary self, which is only one possible form of our primary self among a myriad of others unbeknown to us. It is as though we were the ruler of a country that extends infinitely beyond the horizon but which we have never explored past a familiar enclave we call our little world.

We must concede, however, that our individual experience exposes us to the gradually disabling effect of aging and the risk of injury or illness, which can also decrease our abilities. Besides, the act of defining our individuality through specific choices, as we try to make life meaningful and worthwhile, can become over the years more and more inveterate and restrictive.

So, for all intents and purposes, the opportunity to realize our incredibly vast human potential is lost in part as we age. It is nonetheless safe to assume that much of it remains. In other words, we may consider our habits satisfying, but we should never forget that our nature includes an inborn capacity for adaptation. We can reinvent our individuality in accordance with a wide variety of environments.

Having said this, our ultimate goal in life should never be to exhaust all the desirable possibilities inherent in our nature. Such a goal would be preposterous, as it could never be achieved in a thousand years, let alone during our lifetime. Thus, the only sane and feasible alternative is to take stock of our situation and make the best of it by committing to a worthy path that is consistent with our natural aspirations and abilities, and the opportunities available to us. In short, the point of the matter is not to do everything that is worthwhile but to do a few good and suitable things enjoyably and commendably well.

Summary of Self-Realization:

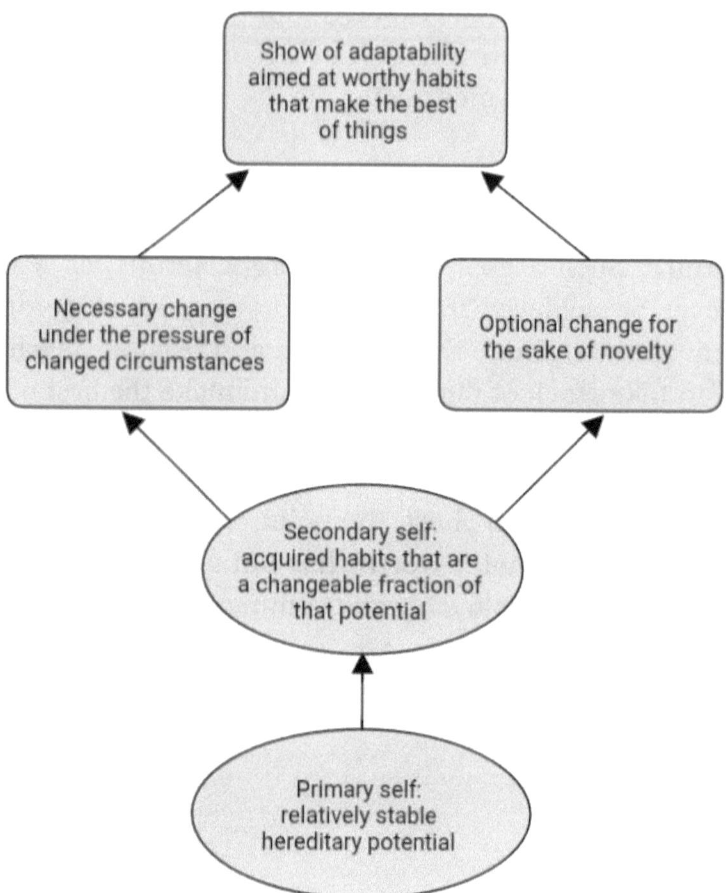

Mental Hygiene

"The art of living is the art of choosing a way of thinking or acting over other such ways."

Let us begin with courage. It is the backbone of every human deed, and for that reason it can be considered a supreme virtue. Now, what is the stuff of courage? Without a doubt, vitality and assurance are integral to it. That is, we cannot find the courage to undertake something unless we feel energetic and capable enough to achieve it. But there is more to courage than having faith in our ability to succeed. There must also be the conviction that a certain goal is worth our best efforts to reach it. Without this conviction our will is faint, and it falters, as it lacks the mental leverage to act decisively.

Therefore, in order to lead an active and rewarding life, we should nurture these known underpinnings of courage, like the ramified root of a plant, to help it grow and flourish. More precisely, we should abide by a healthy lifestyle and acquire a visceral knowledge of our natural aptitudes and predilections by testing ourselves constantly and mindfully in all sorts of experiences. This sound and luminous attitude is the wisdom we need to develop a strong and clear sense of purpose that compels us to take effective action. It should be valued and pursued above all else.

That said, the more our direction in life is definite and resolute, in terms of the principles we adopt and the causes we champion, the more it is exclusive. In the limited framework of time, every yes is a token of commitment to something whose full expression demands a no, as a token of detachment toward everything else. Likewise, we cannot build a home without settling on a preferred combination of location and style that proves both selective and restrictive. Conversely, a vagrant who roams about the world indolently may very well enjoy the utmost freedom, but at the end he has nothing to show for his existence but a rotting corpse.

To sum up, the art of living is the art of choosing a way of thinking or acting over other such ways, and the choices we make illustrate our take on the meaning of life. It is always from this individual perspective that we judge people and things, and view them favorably or not. Some pass muster and enter the intimate circle of our allegiances and some don't, while others are neither out nor in this circle and remain tolerably on the fringe. Whatever the case, the point of this hierarchy is to establish priorities and devote our time and energy to them. The rest is beyond the scope of our personal engagement. Quite simply, it is none of our business.

Still, when we fail to grasp the relative merit of a belief or practice, we should beware of the arrogant tendency to discard it outright as though it were pure garbage. There always exists a particular stance according to which it makes sense or has value. We may not share it with others; yet, beyond this prerogative, we should frame our disagreement in a courteous debate, as we humbly recognize that the absolute truth eludes everyone, even the wisest among us. We all create our own narrative about the alpha and omega of everything, and while we may be knowledgeable to a degree, our partial ignorance is like an open door that allows our fancy to creep into our reason and corrupt it.

Perhaps the best approach is for us to meet peaceably at the crossroads of reality and fiction, and show tolerance on all matters, except the protection of individual freedoms, which applies to everyone and implies mutual respect. This protection must be advocated unequivocally because it correlates with the promotion of social justice or constitutes a necessary bulwark against the regression from the rule of law to the law of the jungle.

This moderate liberalness should moreover prevent the mental sclerosis that happens with age when we become complacently ensconced in our hidebound ways. We need to keep a nimble mind to cope with the changes, big or small, that befall us ineluctably in the course of our existence. In a word, we need to stay adaptable: capable of tapping our wealth of human resources to overcome the illusion of absurdity that may arise in times of adversity. The end of life as we know it is not truly the end of life if we can learn new ways to live meaningfully and joyfully.

Summary of Mental Hygiene:

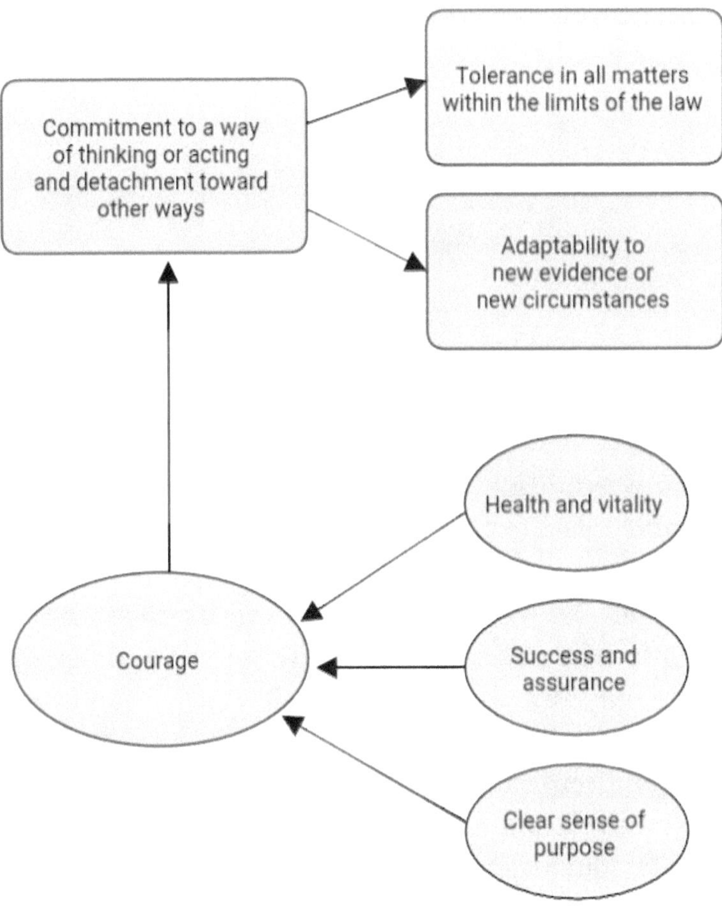

Inner Peace

"Nothing is more excruciating than misery compounded by shame when we fail miserably for lack of trying."

As we all know, our human experience is made of perceptions versus the objects of these perceptions, which refer to our inward or outward reality as distinct from our consciousness. It is a product of interaction and interpretation that is specifically human. Ergo, an evil is only so in relation to our nature and to the degree that it frustrates our desire to live and help others live happily. It reveals our purpose. Furthermore, in our fight against this evil, the battlefield is our mind and the peace we seek is always within.

How we achieve this peace is a matter of strategic thinking. If what frustrates our purpose proves invincible after numerous efforts to the contrary, there comes a time when raising the white flag is the only reasonable option.

This is a personal judgment call where we concede defeat in good conscience because we believe in our heart of hearts that fighting on would be both painful and pointless. We can accept this defeat all the more serenely as we learn to think constructively, bearing in mind our adaptability, that is, our ability to adjust our purpose in a resourceful and meaningful way. While we surrendered on one front, we can win on another. And life goes on, as they say, until the fateful day of our death in battle.

But if what frustrates our purpose can be overcome, the only thing that may keep us from fulfilling this purpose is ourselves, as we are sometimes guilty of laziness or cowardice in the throes of difficulties. These evils lurk like parasites deep inside our character and undermine its strength. They can frustrate our desire to live and help others live happily even more gravely than the worst misfortune. Nothing is more excruciating than misery compounded by shame when we fail miserably for lack of trying. We must leverage our conscience to goad the warrior within and fight the good fight to avoid this hell.

Should we choose to indulge the weaknesses of our character because it is easier and safer than engaging in a difficult struggle, we would increasingly feel so unassured that we would grow chronically lethargic, with only the prospect of regret to haunt our fallow soul. What is worse, we might lapse into cynicism, which is a crafty way of sparing our conscience by denying the value of worthy goals to excuse our passivity. Such is the last refuge of the recreant warrior where he wastes away contemptibly until his final rest.

True inner peace is a function of courage in the line of duty—broadly understood as the areas of personal and moral responsibility that make up our existence. Indeed, we owe it to ourselves, our fellow humans, and ultimately the source of life itself to meet the challenge of living fully, happily, and respectably.

Summary of Inner Peace:

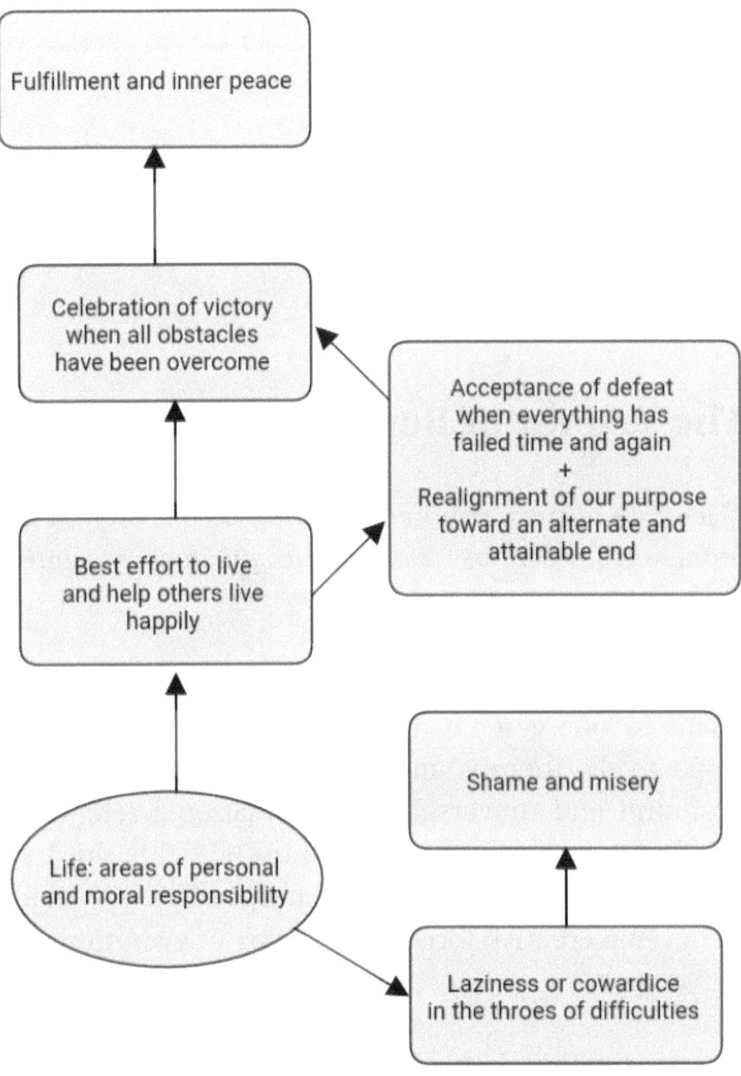

The Trilogy of Being

"The idea of pure random is totally inconsistent with the universal order as a dynamic product of universal evolution."

Beyond our primary self and our secondary self, which relate to our genetic makeup and our acquired habits respectively, there is another level of being that is more profound and universal: our foundational self. Whereas the first two are human and transient, this third self is divine and eternal. Here, the concept of divinity refers to a supreme creative force at the heart of everything in the universe.

The distinction between these three selves is purely analytical. Our nature, while multifaceted, is a unified entity. Therefore, our primary, secondary, and foundational selves are the three distinct but indivisible aspects of our being.

On what basis can we predicate a supreme creative force at the heart of everything in the universe? The answer to this question arises from two observations.

First, the idea of pure random is totally inconsistent with the universal order as a dynamic product of universal evolution. Worse yet, it is intrinsically flawed, because movement without an actuating purpose that aims at a particular outcome makes no sense whatever. As it happens, the universal order reveals a system of invariable laws where bodies move by virtue of their natural tendency toward certain preferred behaviors or states. In other words, this order is the ever-shifting target of an evolutionary arrow that implies some form of determinism.

Second, the oneness of the supreme creative force that inheres in all things—and accounts for the evolution and order of the universe—can be deduced from the oneness of our human nature. We may each experience a host of conflicting desires and feelings, which betray the complexity of our inner life, but we do so as an individual who aspires to resolve these conflicts and achieve harmony. Additionally, we humans comprise every known element or structure of the observable universe, from the simple constituents of atoms to the complex cellular composition of living organisms. And it stands to reason that no chaotic multiplicity of creative forces could beget such a cohesive and inclusive entity as a human being.

What about the eternity of the force in question, which inheres in us as in everything else and is consequently our foundational self? It is hypothesized on the grounds of the following rationale:

There are two different and complementary perspectives from which we can view reality. On the one hand, there is the infinity of interrelated parts that together form the universal whole and may either be inert or alive, and simple (elementary particles) or complex (atoms and multicellular organisms, and everything in between of increasing complexity or size). Our human experience and the science we derive from it—in conditional terms of causes and effects that relate facts and events to their circumstances—are within the bounds of this familiar perspective.

On the other hand, there is the single, omnipresent, and primordial determinant of the rules of causality in the universe. It never manifests the full range of its supreme creative force at any given point in evolution; so it is always partly, if not completely, virtual. As such, it transcends the limits of experience and compounds the mystery of its origin with the mystery of its nature.

This new perspective is less familiar than the previous one because it requires a distillation of reality at a high level of philosophical abstraction. That said, the idea of origin suspiciously mirrors the logic of procreator and offspring that is peculiar to the world of temporal phenomena versus that of their timeless essence. It presumably doesn't apply to this essence and hence creates a bogus problem that can be ignored.

Summary of The Trilogy of Being:

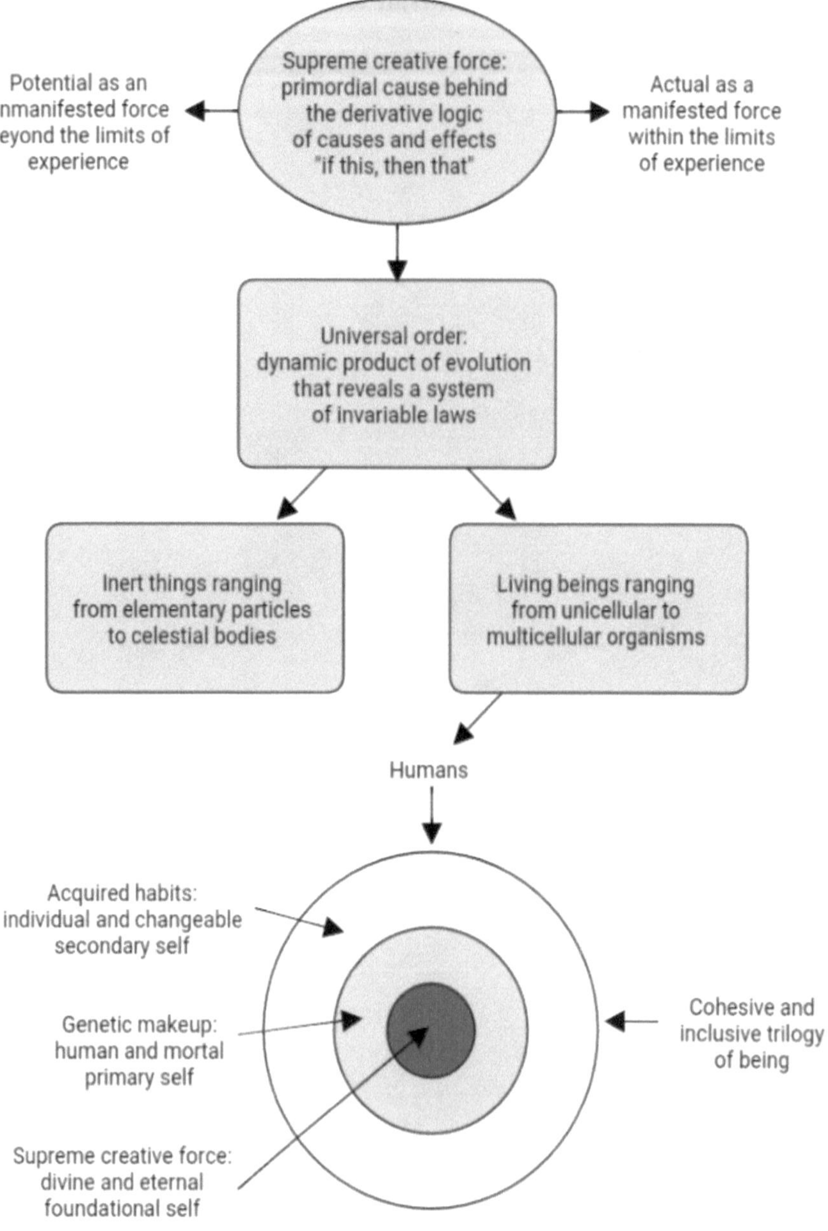

The Nature of Nature

"We are more capable of inquisitively posing questions than of answering them conclusively."

Typically, the inner life of an individual is labeled "subjective" and the outer world, "objective." The former can only be accessed directly by this individual through self-awareness, but can be communicated to others who speak the same language inasmuch as they can identify with the intimate experience confided in them; the latter can be accessed directly by many individuals who share a comparable sensory apparatus and can exchange their observations effectively.

Truth is, we all share a basic humanness that allows both a collective and introspective examination of our common natural attributes. So the principle of objectivity is not only applicable to the outer world but also to our inner life as human beings. In the end, everything—within and without—takes place on a single stage: consciousness, where our inner life and the outer world can equally be taken as objects of study. Perhaps a more appropriate concept to describe any shared body of knowledge is intersubjectivity, because it takes into account this consciousness as a cardinal fact underlying all other facts.

Since the 17th century, natural science has methodically focused on the study of the outer world, treated exclusively as a multifarious object. From this perspective, we are led to view this outer world as a mechanical entity whose behavior can be monitored, theorized, predicted, and often manipulated. Its intimate nature as a multifarious subject—capable of having a subjective experience in an elementary or more advanced way—is kept out of the equation as though it didn't exist.

Admittedly, this universal capacity for subjective experience is a conjectural proposition, lacking the full support of empirical evidence. Yet it is the logical conclusion to this ontological argument: No increase in complexity can explain the emergence of human consciousness, as the most evolved form of subjective experience, if some embryonic capacity for such experience is not present from the outset in the building blocks of evolution. This embryonic capacity is the seed that makes further developments in consciousness possible. To put it differently, the mental inner life of humans cannot be founded on precursory elements that are purely physical or blind to their existence and every other. Similarly, the rules of culture (values that guide behavior) must be compatible with the laws of nature (principles that govern phenomena), even though they are not reducible to them. Otherwise, the world becomes utterly incoherent.

Some may disagree and uphold the idea of radical emergence, according to which the universe was after the Big Bang and for billions of years in a pure state of blind physicality, until a Goldilocks juncture in the course of evolution when a critical threshold of complexity was reached and consciousness was created ex nihilo. Others, however, will deem this idea outlandish or even asinine like the claim that zero multiplied by a number does not equal zero if this number is large enough by some magical order of magnitude.

Incidentally, the creation myth of Abrahamic religions tells a comparable story of divine intervention that miraculously infuses spirit into matter for the creation of man and woman. While it cannot simply be dismissed as impossible, it is arguably quite improbable.

In any case, it is absurd to relegate consciousness to the status of epiphenomenon, as an inconsequential oddity, while the material dimension of the universe is considered the foundation of all existence. Why is it absurd? Because consciousness is in fact the only reality known to us, which includes all the perceptions and conceptualizations of natural science about its staple object of study: the outer world. Furthermore, it is the concept of matter that is the most abstract and elusive, and surely doesn't warrant the hype that pegs it as the foundation of all existence. The only thing we can safely say about matter is that it is the way the outer world appears to us as it opposes a resistance to our free will.

In conclusion, we must acknowledge the true bedrock of our human experience and of the science we derive from it. Most obviously, but also most mysteriously, this true bedrock is consciousness.

This blend of obviousness and mysteriousness is prevalent in every aspect of our existence. What we observe is obviously the way it is, but the reason why it is so, instead of being different or void, is infinitely mysterious. In short, we are reduced to ascertaining everything and explaining nothing. Of course we can relate this to that and develop an understanding of how things work, but again the reason why they work the way they do as opposed to differently or not at all is beyond our ken.

Now, what can we venture to say about the universe to restore the inner side of its nature, while abiding by the standard of credibility based on facts?

Let us answer this question with a brief and tentative theory of consciousness: At the beginning of evolution there is an infinity of subatomic particles in a chaotic cloud. At that subatomic level, consciousness is the simplest, most basic form of subjective experience. With time atoms form, then molecules, then cells, and finally multicellular organisms. At these new, increasingly more complex and integrated levels, a new entity emerges that behaves as one with a unified consciousness (in a remotely similar way, an incoherent and diffuse source of light can become coherent and focused in the form of a laser via optical amplification). For all evolved animals, however, this unified consciousness occurs in a specialized organ, namely the brain, itself hardwired to an assortment of specialized senses like sight and touch.

And the rest of the body? Does it have a lower, fragmented consciousness? This stumper is the blind spot of our self-awareness. It betrays a salient and humbling aspect of our human condition: We are more capable of inquisitively posing questions than of answering them conclusively.

What about highly integrated societies like those of ants, bees, and termites? Are such societies mega-organisms that have a unified consciousness? Perhaps societies in general, and especially the less highly integrated societies of evolved animals like carnivores and primates, lack the cohesive unity of living organisms. If so they never achieve the same existential status as the latter and hence the same level of consciousness. This restriction likely applies to the universe as a whole because of its varied and divided organization. To be honest, these conjectures are a shot in the dark and will probably always be points of contention.

The fact remains that the presence of consciousness across the entire spectrum of physical entities in the universe means they all feel determined to attain their end, be it nonliving or living. In turn, the attainment of this end suggests a feeling of fulfillment. The more complex and integrated a physical entity proves to be, the less rudimental that feeling becomes and conversely. At the top of the evolutionary pyramid, humans can experience a rich array of positive emotions (e.g., pleasure, joy, and pride) whenever their efforts meet with success thanks to their abilities together with relatively favorable circumstances. In human societies, these circumstances include the mutual benefits of solidarity.

As we bring to light, albeit imperfectly, the inner side of the universe, we are setting the stage for an important revelation: The supreme creative force at the heart of creation is likewise a supreme nurturing force that not only introduces things and beings into this temporal world but also provides them with the means to achieve their purpose. It does so within the limits of its immensely resourceful nature that nonetheless leaves room for negative outcomes and the negative feelings they induce, such as pain and suffering in the case of humans and other animals.

This supreme nurturing force is reminiscent of a mother's unconditional love for her child, as she does everything in her power to prepare this child for a successful and joyful life. This love may be unconditional, yet this power is not unlimited. The mother can tragically let her beloved child die before her very eyes, for want of being able to save it.

This revelation is important because it leads to a moral imperative: Live in accordance with the supreme nurturing force within you and honor it with a profound self-love that promotes your well-being. Elevate this self-love to the love of others through solidarity, as your concept of self expands to include the human community where you found a civilized opportunity to enjoy a worthwhile existence. Also, understand your vital dependence on the environment and learn to lovingly protect this second mother of sorts. Do not, however, vacillate when you need to avoid or fight predators, animal or human, that are intractable and threatening in the extreme; your first moral duty is to safeguard your own life force, without which you cannot be a force for good. Still, when at all possible, let universal love be your way of life. There may not be a higher truth, more deserving of our reflective attention and active respect.

Summary of The Nature of Nature:

1. As a conscious event, experience is the primary fact that underlies all other facts

2. "Matter" is a mere abstraction based on the apparent otherness of the outer world as it opposes a resistance to our free will

3. a) Our consciousness is among the emergent properties of life at an advanced stage of evolution that includes the brain
b) These properties are not reducible to those of the subatomic constituents of the brain but logically they must be compatible with them
c) Elementary particules must therefore have a rudimental capacity for subjective experience that remotely foreshadows the advanced consciousness specific to human life at a high level of multicellular complexity
d) With subjective experience comes a sense of fulfillment or nonfulfillment that grows in complexity from simple to complex things and depends on whether or not a given purpose is achieved

4. Life promotes itself in the form of self-love that extends to the love of everything that is necessary for life

5. a) The supreme creative force at the heart of creation is likewise a supreme nurturing force that not only creates things but also provides them with the means to promote themselves successfully within certain limits that leave room for failure
b) This force is mighty but not almighty

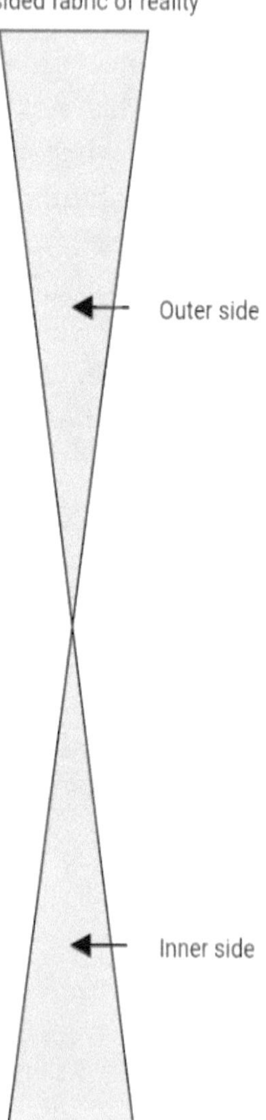

Rationality and Reality

"Aspects of reality are regularly considered in isolation or raised to the status of absolutes, when they ought to be taken as relative parts of a complex totality."

Fragmentation—related to the practice of analysis and the use of language—is a typical downside of rational thought. It distracts us from the interconnectedness of everything and can mislead us into believing that each fragment is real independently from the organic whole to which it belongs.

This downside, however, is also an upside: Whereas our experience cannot be processed intelligibly and usefully as a whole, except in a vague mystical sense, the act of fragmentation divides this experience into easily digestible bits of information, which can serve to construct a clear and practical representation of reality, properly described as an infinite network of distinct elements.

Indeed, this fragmentation can be offset by the willingness to unite these elements to restore their oneness. Yet it remains pervasive and pernicious. Aspects of reality are regularly considered in isolation or raised to the status of absolutes, when they ought to be taken as relative parts of a complex totality. It is of course tempting to indulge our taste for simplicity at the expense of integrity; but resisting this temptation, to prove consistent with both the unity and the complexity of things, is the only and difficult way to the truth.

Alas, the easy and lazy way is the dominant one precisely because it is the path of least resistance. We usually fail to acknowledge the perverse ramifications of analytical and linguistic fragmentation. Alone or together with other factors, intellectual or psychological, like brainwashing and wishful thinking, this product of reason is the root of widespread fallacies.

Here are two telling examples: scores of people view "God," or the principle of all phenomena, living or inert, as separate from the universe, and likewise regard the "soul," or the immaterial core of humans, as separate from the body. This merely constitutes the tip of the iceberg. There is a host of other objects of thought that we routinely abstract from their context as though they made sense on their own. Actually they don't.

To illustrate the universal blend of unity and complexity, let us examine the nature of opposites. This nature is ideally illustrative because opposites are a comprehensive set of cardinal points that hold within their compass every facet of the universe. Most importantly, they invariably come in pairs like the back and front of a single cloth, which here symbolizes the fabric of reality. Furthermore, they represent the diametrical extremes of a continuum that includes a vast array of intermediate degrees. Similarly, black and white are the two poles of the color spectrum with all the hues in between.

Among opposites, identity and alterity have a special status as the archetypal pair. They mark the beginning of the complex universe: a diversified if unified multiplicity of things. Modern cosmology speaks of a Big Bang, accompanied by expansion and cooling, thereby creating conditions for evolution. Prior to this critical juncture, the universe was presumably collapsed into a state of virtuality that amounted to nothing. Or rather, let us say nothing knowable, thus implying that it was still something, albeit mysterious, since it contained the potential for everything.

The question is why did the universe deviate from virtuality to actuality? Perhaps the key to solving this conundrum can be found in the following statistical fact, which reveals a universal law: Extremes are unstable and tend to regress toward the mean. In other words, the dynamics of change that determine a process to top out, then taper off inexorably, are akin to the swing of a pendulum that can never rest at either extremity of the arc it traces, as it gravitates to the middle and moves to and fro with decreasing amplitude until it settles.

This settling, however, or state of maximum entropy, is only true in the case of a closed system—with no external interference. What if the universe was both closed and open by reason of some unknown that prevents maximum entropy? As such, it would forever remain in a state of flux. So in the end, with this new pair of complementary opposites, which represent the two antipodes of a dynamic continuum, the idea of reality as an amalgam of extremes and intermediates comes full circle. Not black, neither white, nor even grey, but a perpetual color variation spanning the whole spectrum.

Summary of Rationality and Reality:

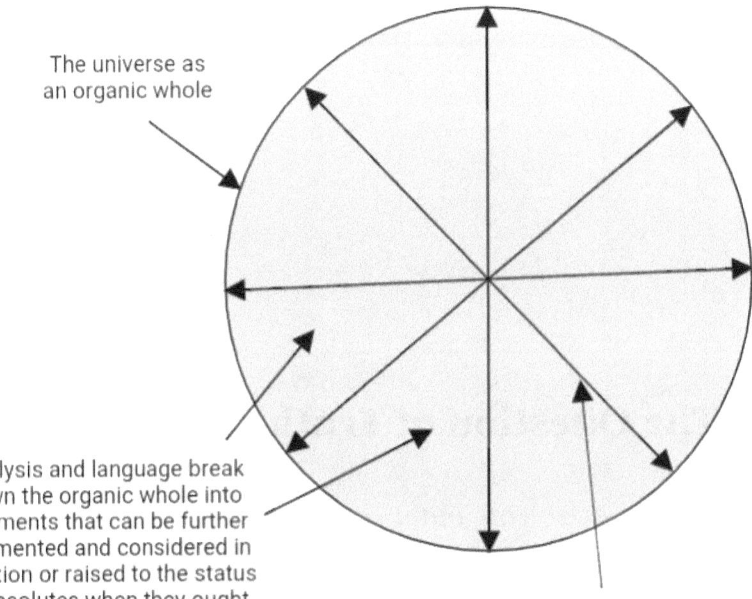

The Question of Truth

"There exists an outer reality whose nature we must grasp through effective representation. Our survival is at stake."

When dealing with the concept of truth we must frame the question as follows: Since reality, as far as we are concerned, takes place nowhere but in the mind as an object of perception, what is the nature of this essential stage on which rests any hope of seeing the truth about reality?

There are two opposite and complementary viewpoints from which we can describe the mind: the inner side, made of mental states, and the outer side, made of neurobiological processes. Neither causes the other, although changes in mental states always accompany changes in neurobiological processes and vice versa.

These states and processes show the two-sided if unified nature of the mind.

In all likelihood, the universe as a whole—which includes the mind plus an evolutionary process leading to it by degrees from the most simple to the most complex things—presents the same fundamental characteristic. Here, the implicit hypothesis is that there exists both a universal inner side and a universal outer side that together form the universal whole as a dual but unitary system. Of course it must be understood that these two sides vary in tandem proportionally to the level of simplicity or complexity of each thing.

Let us start with the following definition of truth: a faithful representation of the outer reality by our inner self. According to science, this representation is a mental construct based on sensory stimuli that provide different clues—visual, auditory, olfactory, gustatory, or tactile—about the presence of physical things in the world, as parts of this multiple world or components of complex things. In short, it is a translation of the language of reality in the language of our sensitivity. Beyond that, further translations ensue in various human languages, including mathematics.

In what sense can these translations be true to their model (i.e., reality itself from a physical perspective)? Two examples shall help us answer this question: A dog as we see it with the naked eye and the English word "dog" have nothing in common morphologically, and neither does a protein as seen through a microscope and the English word "protein." But that, for all intents and purposes, is secondary. Of great import, however, is how a dog and a protein relate to their environment, in all manner of behaviors, and what physical features they have, from a structural and functional viewpoint. And it so conveniently happens that these behaviors and these physical features, which reveal the nature of this dog and this protein, are equally expressible by any standard body of symbols. The same can be said of everything else in the universe, provided it enters our field of consciousness via our senses, augmented or not by scientific instruments.

That said, isn't the language of our sensitivity versus human languages likely to be morphologically closer to the reality of its physical model? It could therefore be an analog that is capable of yielding immediate and practical information about size, shape, and consistency, among other aspects. Admittedly, analog is here a questionable abstraction, because we have no direct access to this model, ergo no direct knowledge of it. What is more, the outer reality in itself is, strictly speaking, an empty concept with no experimental foundation and validity. These objections notwithstanding, this abstraction and this concept remain useful in implying that there exists an outer reality whose nature we must grasp through effective representation. Our survival is at stake.

What about the inner reality and the issue of truth in this new context? If we restrict the scope of this question to our conscious inner life, or the direct experience of our feelings and thoughts ("direct" meaning absent any mental translation natively posing a problem of accuracy), the answer appears straightforward at first blush. Yet, when we consider our formidably complex interiority—including impulses that we manifest unawares under the guise of reasonableness—the pursuit of self-knowledge becomes an ambitious task strewn with pitfalls.

Worse still, if we apply the notion of inner reality to everything in the universe, this formidable complexity is compounded by impenetrable mystery, as we have no direct experience of any interiority but our own. We can nonetheless conjecture that in every case things have some form of consciousness ranging from the most elementary to the most evolved.

Some may argue that our mind's unconscious component provides evidence of a more primitive manifestation than its conscious counterpart. They may consequently suggest that unconsciousness precedes consciousness evolutionarily. Upon further examination, however, the opposite argument seems more credible.

Picture a crew that works autonomously in the bowels of a modern ship to maintain and operate it under the captain's command. This hierarchy—exhibiting two main levels of responsibility—is a token of nautical advancement and sophistication, compared with a prehistoric log raft that a single *Homo Erectus* crudely propels. Likewise, we humans are the product of a long evolution that led initially to unicellular organisms and eventually to multicellular ones, equipped with specialized senses, organs, and limbs, plus a multifaceted nervous system.

The part of our life that is unaware only receives this qualifier from the part that is aware, which we readily call our self. It derives from our highly evolved, complex organization, consisting of two major and interdependent tiers: the bottom one is our body and subconscious brain, tantamount to a life-support system, as it automatically handles a multiplicity of vital processes, which are either physiological or psychological. Like the crew to its captain in the above example, it answers to the conscious brain, the top tier, where we devise strategies to meet the challenge of living healthily and happily.

Now, as a map of sorts, what schematic image of the universe can we draw, based on our speculations about the outer and inner reality, and the relationships between things? A few lines of thought come to mind. Everything arises from a combination of environmental opportunities and natural potentialities. The proximate environment is contingent on a remote environment, which is itself contingent on a faraway environment and so on and so forth infinitely. Everything is therefore a function of the interactions it has with everything else; its nature is one with the entire universal network to which it belongs. Yet, while everything is identical in terms of the range of these interactions, there is one significant feature that makes each thing intimately distinct from every other. This feature is the unique perspective each thing has on the universal network, given its particular form, place, and time.

Summary of The Question of Truth:

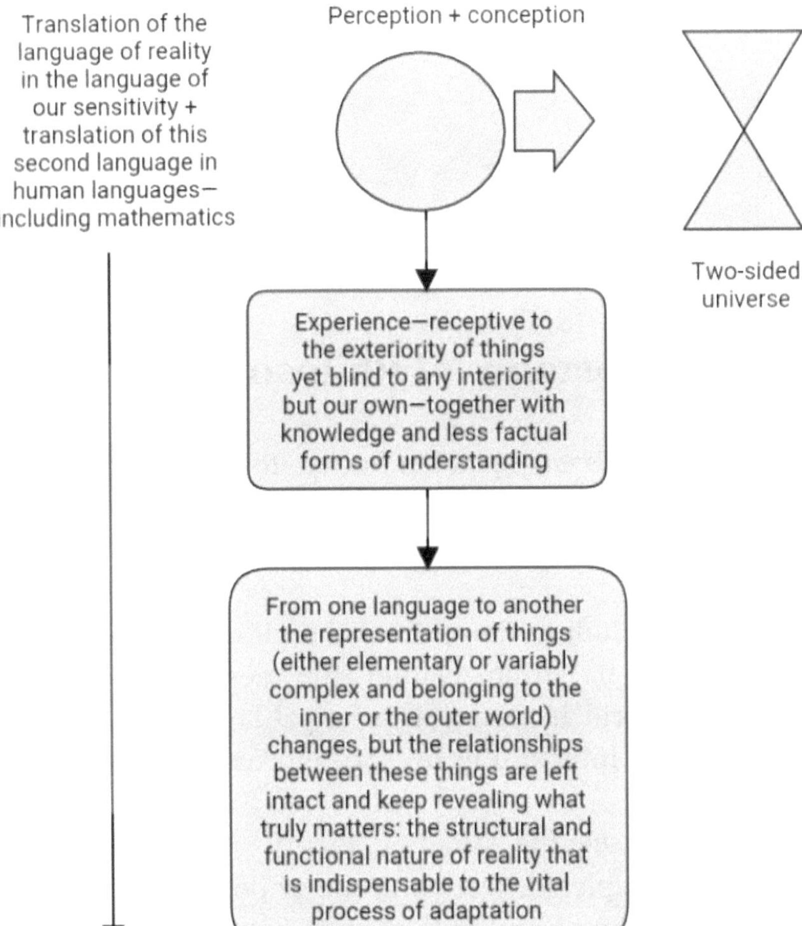

The Importance of Philosophy

"Philosophy is an open invitation to think profoundly about things and dialogue respectfully with others in order to enjoy a mutual enrichment of ideas."

Science—including the general theories that provide the conceptual backdrop behind the description of the material world in terms of universal laws—is inherently incapable of infusing our lives with meaning and value.

Some may see the scientific theory of evolution as a counterexample. In fact, it is the philosopher Friedrich Nietzsche who perverted the law of natural selection into a rule of social domination where might is right (in fairness to Nietzsche, we should qualify this statement to match the scope and richness of his thought, which also advocates the sublimation of one's power over others through self-mastery; but this elaboration belongs elsewhere in academic works on the subject).

Perhaps the line between science and philosophy will be blurred when the former officially takes as objects of study both the material world of phenomena and the immaterial world of consciousness. At any rate, it is philosophy together with religion that aims at creating a comprehensive ideological framework for working out the first principles governing the universe, and also for understanding the purpose of life and laying down rules of conduct.

Note that religion is at heart a philosophy whose highly suspicious claim is that, contrary to a human construct, it is revealed by "God" and is absolutely true, beyond debate. Philosophy, on the other hand, is never expounded under a pretense of absolute truth; it is a system of thought that is never certain, however convincing it may be thanks to a reasonable and credible argumentation. Yet, in spite of this irreducible doubt, anyone who cares to rise above the mechanical rut of a genetically and socially programmed automaton will not put in question the worthiness of the philosophical endeavor.

Why is philosophy irreducibly uncertain? Because no amount of evidence can ever guarantee the unquestionable veracity of an ideological framework whose only token of reasonableness and credibility is its compatibility with facts. And this compatibility cannot exclude the possibility of another ideological framework that is also compatible with facts. The only criteria left to decide between the two are either a question of cultural sensitivity or a matter of simplicity and elegance against a tortuous and awkward rival that seems thus by reason of significant shortcomings.

There is a kinship between philosophy and poetry, since all philosophical systems of thought never perfectly mirror the nature of things, although the ones and the other surely overlap to some meaningful and valuable extent. In similar fashion, a metaphor is never identical to what it represents figuratively but is only comparable to it; both share some fundamental characteristics that justify this restricted comparison. And so philosophy is an art whose product could be dubbed the poetry of meaning and value.

There are no grounds for confrontational arrogance in this discipline, only for humility and receptiveness. All in all, philosophy is an open invitation to think profoundly about things and dialogue respectfully with others in order to enjoy a mutual enrichment of ideas.

From a personal standpoint, every philosophical discourse can be encapsulated in a single interjection: Look! The onus is on the listener or reader to survey with the purity of a child every example of the universal unfolding and reach an enlightened *ah!* moment. This enlightenment is an intimate grasp of reality beyond the words that merely point to it like fingers. Hence, words are not the knowledge itself but signs that guide our minds to a sense of what is in its immediacy. They are a stepping stone, a reason for acquainting ourselves quietly and deeply with the world through observation and reflection. We must always remember that by themselves they amount to nothing more than sounds or marks. In short, the map is not the journey in our pilgrimage to knowledge.

Actually, of all the books available to curious minds striving to unveil the nature of things, the most important one cannot be found in libraries and bookstores. What is more, it is not made up of words but of the things themselves as we experience them. And this book is none other than our very existence as a repository of facts and events that should be regular objects of meditation, leading to profound insights about reality.

Summary of The Importance of Philosophy:

The Divine Magician

"What is ordinary and dull to the average mind, numbed by knowledge, is in fact an extraordinary example of divine wizardry, forever creating something out of nothing."

Let us begin with the law of causality: Given these circumstances surrounding this object, we obtain this outcome in all probability. That is what experience teaches us through observation.

Why is it so? To answer this question we must leave the world of empirical evidence and enter the world of speculative reason, dealing with the intangible. If the first world is physical, the second is metaphysical. There we no longer talk about the behavior of things but about the force determining this behavior, like the unseen hand animating a puppet. And it is worth noting that the concept of force in science is no less abstract than the concept of God or universal principle in religions and philosophy, even though the former differs from the latter in that it applies to the behavior of particular objects in specific circumstances instead of applying indeterminately to the workings of the entire universe. It is therefore considerably more precise and practical, allowing predictions and manipulations that are integral to the development of technology and the advancement of humanity.

That said, scientific progress is often accompanied by regress, as technological innovations both promote and threaten our collective survival. Indeed, the mythical fall of man is the preamble to a bittersweet story of knowledge and responsibility marred by errors and faults.

Let us now return to the law of causality, both framed in empirical evidence (if this, then that, e.g., water boils when heated to 100°C) and speculative reason (this is so because of that: the first law of thermodynamics in the above example, where heat is transferred from a burner to the water through conduction, then dissipated by this water through convection, toward entropy or a state of thermal equilibrium). That is how science describes and explains things, as part of its mechanistic view of the universe whose most remarkable and effective mode of expression is the language of mathematics.

What about the law of causality when framed in speculative reason that is not scientific but religious or philosophical? It then accounts for all empirical evidence with a single, unaccountable notion that is little more than a useless tautology: Things are the way they are because God or the universal principle is such that they are so. No mathematical formulas here, just the verbal language of the most basic and profound logical assumption: The universe cannot be without the power to be, and this power is what the notion of God or universal principle essentially refers to.

Truth is, even the insightful and useful formalism of science, which precisely elicits the outer logic of things, comes short of a total explanation exhausting the universal mystery. First, this formalism, however insightful and useful it is, ignores a dimension of reality that is critical to understanding the universe, namely the inner and immaterial side of things. Second, it amounts to a description of how things work, and this description in turn can serve to make predictions and manipulations, but it doesn't really have an explanatory value. Like religious and philosophical verbalizations about the first cause, it is somewhat tautological: Things are the way they are because their nature is such that they are so. Why is this nature what it is instead of different or void? This question is forever doomed to remain unanswered.

In the end, we are faced with a universe that is shrouded in mystery, no matter how well we may objectively decipher its physical nature or intuitively fathom its immaterial essence. Moreover, although our observations and theorizations may give us a sense of familiarity regarding the way things are, we should never lose our sense of wonder. What is ordinary and dull to the average mind, numbed by knowledge, is in fact an extraordinary example of divine wizardry, forever creating something out of nothing.

Consider every new thing, every second of every day: a thought, a word, a gesture, an arrangement or happening of some sort, whatever. Acknowledge the fact that, prior to its occurrence, it was nowhere to be found. And yet, voilà! out of this nowhere—in the intervening space between old things—comes the new thing, like a dove out of an empty hat. Magic!

The universe is but the necessary stage and apparatus for this magic show. As for our knowledge of the show, it is a description of the chain of events and an explanation of this chain in the form of rules that together leave the secret of the magic unbroken. Yes we are aware of the empty hat and the dove that flies out of it, not to mention a host of other relevant things; we have words for each of them, plus ideas and equations to discuss the order of their appearance; but with all that we still walk out of the show scratching our heads, unless we are foolish enough to think that our knowledge is on par with the divine magician who has wowed the child within us.

Summary of The Divine Magician:

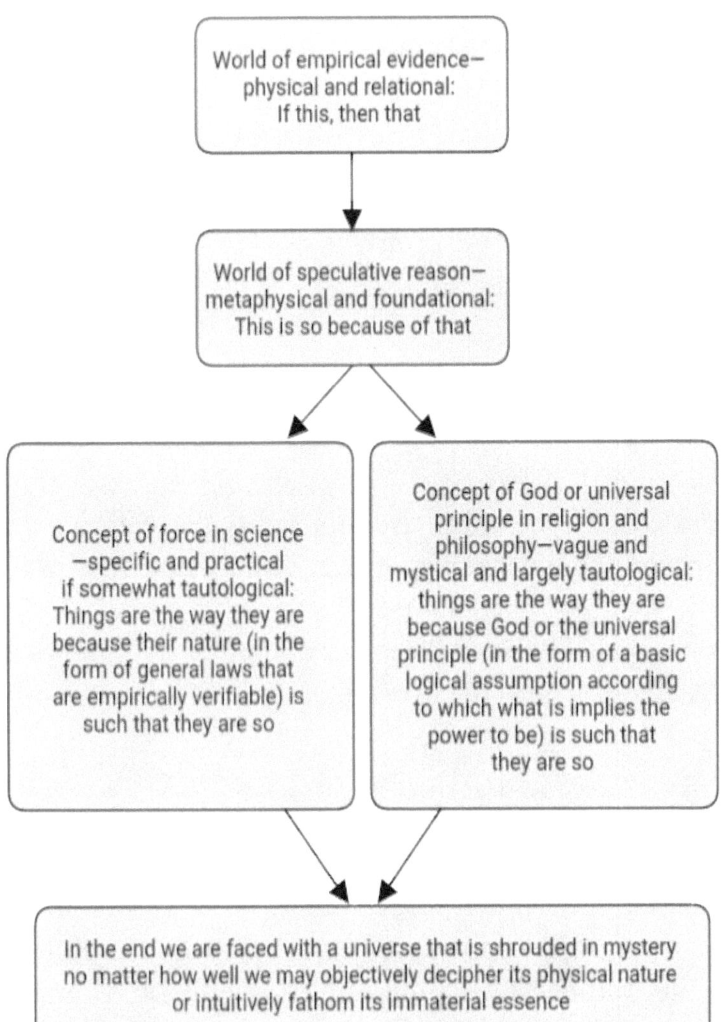

The Art of Living

"The wind of change is only contrary relative to the adverse angle of your mindset, comparable to a sail."

As we look back at the succession of events we have experienced and memorized, the way we view our life depends on how we process it.

The processing is done by a manner of program of our own design, although we often fail to acknowledge our responsibility as the programmer. What is this program? It is none other than our attitude based on our philosophy of life, which determines our outlook on things. The processor, on the other hand, is our very mind where the program performs a set of instructions that transform our immediate sensory experiences into subjective value judgments. How we feel about reality is a reflection of how positive or negative our attitude happens to be.

More precisely, even though we all start with a sphere of influence, proportional to the effect of our mental and physical presence on the world, we cannot in the end control the way things work nor the way people think and act, but we can control our attitude toward them to attain maximum peace and happiness. At best, our life becomes an uplifting story that testifies to our resourcefulness and mindfulness in the art of turning unfavorable situations to good account, as well as savoring the advantages of good fortune.

When devising our attitude, there are some important elements that must be considered and which will shape the way we process reality. These important elements can be divided into two main categories: 1) the things we strive to acquire or achieve to improve our situation and feel energetic, successful, and content; and 2) the things we cultivate within that promote our dignity and serenity no matter what.

First on the list of worthy objectives that deserve our best efforts is health. It is the ground upon which every other worthy objective—like success in a chosen career, relationship, sport, or hobby—is built. In tandem with these objectives are valuable lessons that represent a wise approach to the many challenges of life:

- Beware of the illusion that you shall be happy once this or that is acquired or achieved. You live in the present that is always changing, whereas the past and the future are a present that is gone or one that is coming; they add up to nothing but a memory or a dream. If you are not happy now, you risk being forever unhappy because it is now or possibly never that you will learn to find happiness in the present. So enjoy the journey as you pride yourself on the victory of every forward step but also on the wisdom gained in every fall toward a steady gait. View whatever destination you set as a short pause where you sit less than set yet another destination and so on and so forth until death, which is the only true and lasting rest.

- Do not indulge your negativity bias that arises from your innate oversensitivity to trouble and danger. Make a concentrated effort to look past the negative while keeping it in sight with a realistic and constructive stance. Embrace the positive to foster your attachment to life and bolster your commitment to everything and everyone you love.

- Promptly question any dreary narrative that tars your entire existence with the same brush. A situation rarely warrants our tendency to dramatize as though it was all gloom and doom. Do not allow the bad to keep you down; always strive to bounce back by focusing on the good and the possibilities therein. The wind of change is only contrary relative to the adverse angle of your mindset, comparable to a sail. Adjust this mindset appropriately and it will propel you toward new horizons that are both intimidating and promising. In other words, when facing a situation that dashes your hopes of enjoying the things you love, choose to switch your perspective from obstacle to opportunity. Start imagining what potential for happiness this situation still holds and how you can actualize this potential thanks to some favorable adaptation.

- Recognize the absurdity of fantasizing about a "perfect life" that is free from struggle and suffering. Such perfection actually amounts to boredom and death. Life is by definition a perpetual tension between the state of want and that of satisfaction, in a world that presents an infinite number of difficulties; and the result of this twofold condition is the necessity for exertion and the possibility of frustration. Eliminate all that and you also eliminate everything that is exciting and gratifying in life. Worse still, you eliminate life itself.

- Pick love, not fear, as the driving force behind your decisions. Love vitalizes, whereas fear paralyzes, and there can only be regret and sadness in prolonged idleness. Choose wisely the objects of your commitment, according to your affinities and abilities, and give your best in whatever you do. Be equally resolute and prudent, and always be ready to break the frown of your serious-mindedness with humor and laughter to avoid the foolery of self-importance.

- Experience dignity and serenity by being consistent with your principles through noble choices and valiant efforts. Do the right thing and take credit for it, while acknowledging your debt of gratitude toward the creative and nurturing force at the heart of everything, you included. This force gave you life and the means to live it.

- When you are unhappy, do not blame others to spare your pride and avoid undertaking the necessary efforts to remedy the situation. Instead, empower yourself to overcome your unhappiness by accepting responsibility. Be mindful of the bright side of people and things; be thankful it brightens your days and be happier for it.

By adopting a positive attitude we ensure that we process our experience constructively in order to be joyful. And isn't that our natural aspiration, to fill our heart with joy? But again, that requires a wholesome art of living that can be summed up in one word: wisdom.

Summary of The Art of Living:

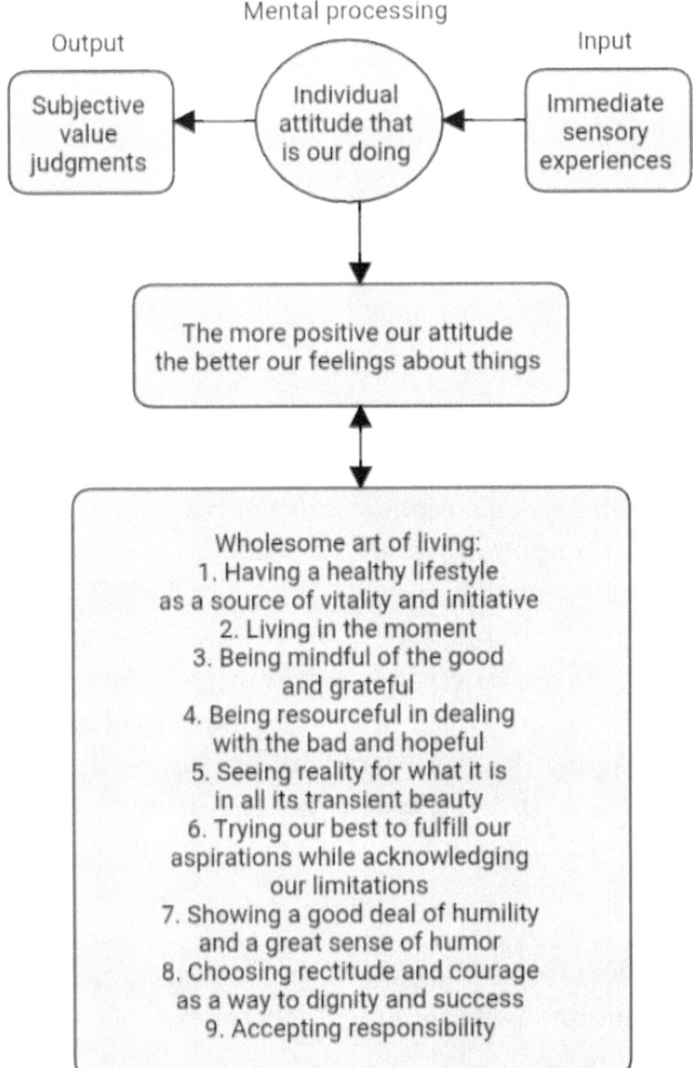

The Exercise of Wonder

"We should make a regular habit of reserving some quiet time to thoughtfully and thankfully review everything that renders our life possible."

There is always an upside and a downside, and we should mindfully acknowledge both into the broadest possible view. Neither the ignorant child, who sees everything through rose-tinted glasses, nor the disillusioned adult, who thinks everything is gloom and doom, can be regarded as wise.

Take for example the natural process of habituation. As things become familiar and largely predictable, we in turn become increasingly insensitive to them. Our focus then shifts predominantly to other things that are, by contrast, unfamiliar and largely unpredictable. Admittedly, the natural process of habituation is a good strategy for managing our consciousness, which is a limited resource that can be overwhelmed with excessive stimulation. It is bad also nonetheless because it dulls our mind and proportionately weakens our capacity for wonder toward the multitude of beneficial things that we have grown accustomed to. In a word, we take them for granted instead of appreciating their positive contribution to our existence.

To offset this unwelcome aspect of the process in question, we should make a regular habit of reserving some quiet time to thoughtfully and thankfully review everything that renders our life possible in all the human ways we are viscerally attached to. In doing so, we can expect our sense of identity and satisfaction to deepen and expand considerably.

As we take stock of the many beneficial things that help us lead a satisfying existence, we should proceed from the ground up, so to speak, beginning with the supreme power that drives the creation and evolution of everything. This power is beyond all religious or philosophical persuasions; it unites them in the primal notion of a founding principle that is the generative, albeit mysterious force behind every past, present, or future phenomenon in the universe.

Science has methodically documented the rules of its outer manifestations while remaining blind to its inner dimension, which must be understood in the most inclusive and elusive fashion, as it contains and exceeds our human experience. Ultimately, no one can be unaware and fail to be in awe of this founding principle without betraying a subhuman level of reflection.

Next in the hierarchy of beneficial things that deserve our utmost attention and appreciation is this twofold reality: 1) the environment that we depend on for our survival, and 2) the community to which we belong, as we stand in solidarity with others to face the challenge of living an enjoyable and meaningful life. This twofold reality is indeed of great benefit, despite the rigors and iniquities that we may suffer along the way. It should inspire us to act more respectfully and kindly toward everything and everyone in the world around us.

Integral to the gift of civilization, bestowed upon us, is a flawed yet advanced level of government, industry, culture, science, and technology. This affords us a privileged opportunity to become paragons of human greatness who shine like beacons with outstanding probity, benevolence, expertise, wisdom, and happiness.

Had we been raised in isolation and allowed to survive without love, save the minimum amount of assistance to help us through the tender age, our human potential would have been sadly reduced to that of a beast. As civilized beings, our calling is to try our best to become these paragons of human greatness.

Summary of The Exercise of Wonder:

The more familiar and predictable things are, the more we incline to take them for granted in a mindless and ungrateful way

↓

We should regularly take time to thoughtfully and thankfully review every aspect of our life that makes it possible and worth living:
1. the creative and nurturing force at the heart of everything
2. the environment that we depend on for our survival
3. the community to which we belong and that shares with us the burden of overcoming difficulties and living fully

↓

Privileged opportunity to grow into individuals of superior character and wisdom who shine with goodness and cheerfulness

Return to the Stream

"The dry stillness of our limited abstractions are also obstructions to the natural flow of things that forever escapes our grasp like running water."

Among the concepts that we use while thinking, talking, or writing about our life, the concept of self (versus the selves of other people and the different entities around us that we can hardly identify with) is clearly pivotal.

How faithful is this concept to our pure experience of living, unmediated by intellectual constructs? This question is definitely worth asking in the spirit of the scientific method, which requires that any hypothesis be empirically and repeatedly tested. We can easily be lulled into an erroneous belief without a second thought if it has a vague semblance of believability. It then resembles a mirage that looks real yet blinds us to the sober facts.

So let us return to the stream of life, away from the dry stillness of our limited abstractions. These abstractions are also obstructions to the natural flow of things that forever escapes our grasp like running water. No amount of mental clutching will ever stop this flow, which can quench our thirst for life without a bitter aftertaste, provided we are in step with it by learning to let go and move on. The underlying wisdom here is a plea for awareness and adaptability.

Change is not an imperfection that we should fight stubbornly, like the "great" Gatsby (in the novel of the same name) who tragically failed to repeat the past and died trying. It is merely a challenge calling for an appropriate mindset to meet it squarely with a vibrant and pliant resourcefulness that matches the changeful course of the divine creative force within and without us.

To be more precise, how can we faithfully describe our fluid reality devoid of intellections? Perhaps the following description will suffice: It is a medley of transient perceptions, sensations, and emotions that does not constitute an isolated existential path but a crossroads where all aspects of our complex relationship with the world intersect. This medley offers a unique perspective that is very much our own and therefore justifies the concept of self in proportion to this uniqueness. Furthermore, it is an unstable mental expression of our stable genetic information, which is also very much our own, adding weight to the concept of self.

What about our unique perspective with regard to our personal memories, imaginings, and thoughts? Depending on how forgetful and artful we are in remembering the past or envisioning the future, and how conservative or progressive we are in devising our views, this facet of our nature changes with time significantly or not. In the case of our views, the inveterate resistance to change may denote a hidebound reluctance to learn in spite of inconsistencies between these views and reality. We are then partly or largely deluded.

Having said this, is there no room for immutability in the pursuit of truth? That is, embedded in the inescapable transience of things, is there not some permanent core like a motionless axle at the center of a rotating wheel? Arguably there is and the notion of an ultimate and timeless power that inheres in every worldly manifestation is truly warranted. And since we logically include this power as a higher self, we are both mortal, in terms of our human form, and eternal, in terms of our divine foundation. Likewise, a wave apparently rises and falls but essentially remains as the watery matrix from which it emerges, before merging back into this matrix, open to an infinity of rises and falls that punctuate the endless passage of time.

Summary of Return to the Stream:

The self

1. Unique stream of perceptions and feelings that is intimately connected to the world in perpetual flux
2. Unique mix of recollections and imaginings that imperfectly and variably reflects our experience and disposition
3. Unique mix of conceptions and inklings that are all the more peaceful and faithful to reality if they are in step with the flow of things versus clinging bitterly to the past with stubborn denial and wishful thinking
4. Unique genetic makeup that defines our potential for development and fulfillment until death
5. Unique source of being and time that constitutes our foundation and defines the potential for universal creation and evolution

The Eternal Now

"We never lose anything other than a transitory form whose foundation can be neither gained nor lost."

The present should be construed in two ways: as the time being and as the gift of existence.

1) The present is concrete; it is our only means of experience and discovery. By contrast, the past and the future are mere abstractions, stored inside our retentive and imaginative mind like faded photographs and fancied pictures in a drawer.

Always changing, the present is a constant alternation of virtuality and actuality where every form provides the opportunity for the spontaneous creation of a new one out of nothing, insofar as this new form was purely virtual or nowhere actual within the old one before it was created. This nothing—which is still something as the source of everything—is logically deduced but radically unknown. In fact, it exceeds the mundane intellectual framework to which the concept of something is related. Reverence and silence are in the end the only appropriate ways to address it.

We should keep in mind that our multiple and unstable universe cannot be considered separately from the generative nothing that brought it into being. The two are relative to each other or make no sense on their own. They constitute a pair of cosmic dancers that forever testify to their undying intimacy through a stirring tango.

In a nutshell, the art of living is the awareness of our changeful life and the willingness to dance with it. Like a paper boat in the current, we should flow with the present unreservedly.

A word of caution, however. Not clinging to things to avoid suffering can prove self-destructive if it amounts to detaching ourselves from everything. We cannot run away from our life except by heading off a cliff.

The reasonable approach to the problem of clinging gives precedence to our need for self-preservation over the inevitability of change, which is both secondary and critical. Life should not be renounced but accepted for what it is: changeful yet desirous of asserting itself within the bounds of its nature and circumstances. Therefore, the act of letting go should not be a cowardly act of defection or treason toward life, while we are called to champion the cause of freedom, health, wisdom, peace, and happiness, for ourselves and others. Rather, it should be the act of resourcefully adapting to change in a courageous effort to make the best of life. And that implies the good sense to refrain from hankering after the impossible, which is a sure and foolish way of creating our own misery.

2) The present, including our life and our inborn adaptability that enable us to grow and blossom into self-fulfilled adults, we did not bestow upon ourselves. It was mediated by our parents but primarily generated by the founding power at the core of our being (although the opposition between our human self and our foundational self is entirely conceptual as a product of analysis. There is one inclusive, unified self, that lends itself to the above distinctions).

So the impression of loss at every turn of our changeful life—death being the ultimate change—is partly an illusion. In fact, we never lose anything other than a transitory form whose foundation can be neither gained nor lost. The core of our being, from which we can develop time and again within our lifetime and beyond, remains eternally. And what to think of a transitory form that keeps vanishing like a wave into another wave and so on and so forth, with all the waves sharing the same watery soul? Not much really, especially since indefinite sameness would be infinite boredom. Let it flow, my friends, with love and abandon, and may you find peace and happiness in the fully embraced moment, ever-renewed.

Summary of The Eternal Now:

1. The present as the time being

a) It is our only means of experience and discovery
b) It is always changing with each stage providing
the opportunity for the creation of the next stage
out of nothing—the occult potential for everything—
insofar as this next stage did not exist before it
came to be
c) The art of living is the awareness of our changeful
life and the willingness to relinquish the past while
embracing the present thanks to effective adaptations
that afford us a new lease on truth and happiness

2. The present as the gift of existence

a) We sprung into life and adaptability from the
generative nothing that accounts for everything
b) We never lose anything other than a transitory form—
of being, of thought, or behavior—whose generative
foundation can never be gained nor lost

The Spontaneity of Being

"Secular accounts for the way of nature beget a new breed of understanding that portrays the mainspring of all phenomena as a deterministic and evolutionary force that inheres in these phenomena."

Humanity is gradually entering a phase of spiritual and intellectual maturity, though unfortunately at a snail's pace. On the moral front, every imperative traditionally associated with great religions can be derived from the rules of social organization. A pivotal example of such imperatives is this broad commandment: You shall do no harm to others.

Since the Age of Enlightenment and the establishment of liberal democracies, these imperatives have become laws as logical offshoots of this root principle: the defense of individual liberties. Essentially, everyone's freedom hinges on the respect by one another of their respective freedoms. This means that each member of society is required to abstain from violating the inalienable right of fellow members to freely pursue whatever they value above all else—fellow members whose complementary duty is to show the same abstention. Those who disregard this basic requirement are dubbed outlaws who have to suffer the clout of law enforcers.

Thanks to this enlightened form of political system that promotes human rights (as opposed to oppressive monarchies or dictatorships that alienate the people), and thanks to modern strides in human knowledge, including science and technology, the traditional reliance on great religions to reveal a Creator that guides our conscience and explains reality, in all its complexity, is giving way for a growing number of men and women to a type of naturalism that places the cause and purpose of everything squarely within the limits of the world as we know it, empirically and theoretically.

In this revolutionized context, great religions are increasingly regarded as a fanciful construct, a token of cultural infancy akin to breast milk that we can wean ourselves from by finding spiritual and intellectual sustenance in philosophy and science.

In short, secular accounts for the way of nature beget a new breed of understanding that portrays the mainspring of all phenomena as a deterministic and evolutionary force that inheres in these phenomena. By contrast, religious accounts suspiciously portray this mainspring as an anthropomorphic and patriarchal Creator who stands apart from his creation like a watchmaker from the watches he makes (Christ, as the incarnation of God on Earth, is an exception in the biblical narrative that conveys the idea of divine immanence versus transcendence).

Thus, the secular mind no longer views the way of nature as the deliberate execution of a grand design by a rational god of infinite power and wisdom. Instead, it views this way as the spontaneous adventure of a creative principle that is incredibly ingenious but has no innate knowledge. This principle combines a random process of trial and error with a determined process of internal selection that follows a specific orientation, comprising attractors along two major lines: inert things and living beings.

Introspectively, this worldview feels intuitively correct because it matches our own innocent youth, as we learn from our mistakes to live more effectively and happily until the day we die. This time of inexperience and ignorance that we progressively but never completely outgrow is not passed alone, unassisted. We stand in solidarity with our elders whose guidance expedites our learning process. Indeed, life is a story of both competition and cooperation between living beings, with outward experimentation and internal selection completing the storyline.

When we study the beginning of life on Earth, nearly 4 billion years ago, our attention is initially drawn to the turbulent circumstances that surrounded the appearance of the first unicellular life forms—namely bacteria—in the primordial ocean, which then extensively covered the Earth's crust. Most notably we count among these circumstances salvos of asteroids, comets, and meteors hurtling from outer space, fierce electrical storms and ultraviolet radiation in the Earth's atmosphere, together with constant volcanic eruptions, underwater and above, that besieged the planet. In brief, this was a violently unstable period.

To help conceptualize the extraordinary character of this rough beginning, let us examine a simple yet powerful metaphor found in thermodynamics: convection cells. Under certain conditions, a heated liquid forms dissipative structures—made of large bubbles—that are reminiscent of living cells. These structures remain in a state of dynamic equilibrium as long as the heat is maintained. So what started as a cause of disturbance in a liquid at rest becomes instrumental to the appearance of a new form of order that quite remarkably integrates this cause into a lively mode of being. The significance of external energy thereupon changes from destructive to constructive. Likewise, the intrinsic genius of life consists in its ability to feed on the instability of its environment to keep regenerating itself, thereby converting this instability into a source of sustainability.

Human wisdom is a mindful compliance with this intrinsic genius, a disposition to adopt a positive attitude in the face of difficulties and stay adaptable: capable of turning a bad situation to good account. In the end, the noise of contrary forces—that are unsettling at the outset—is transfigured through various adjustments into the harmony of a meaningful existence.

Summary of The Spontaneity of Being:

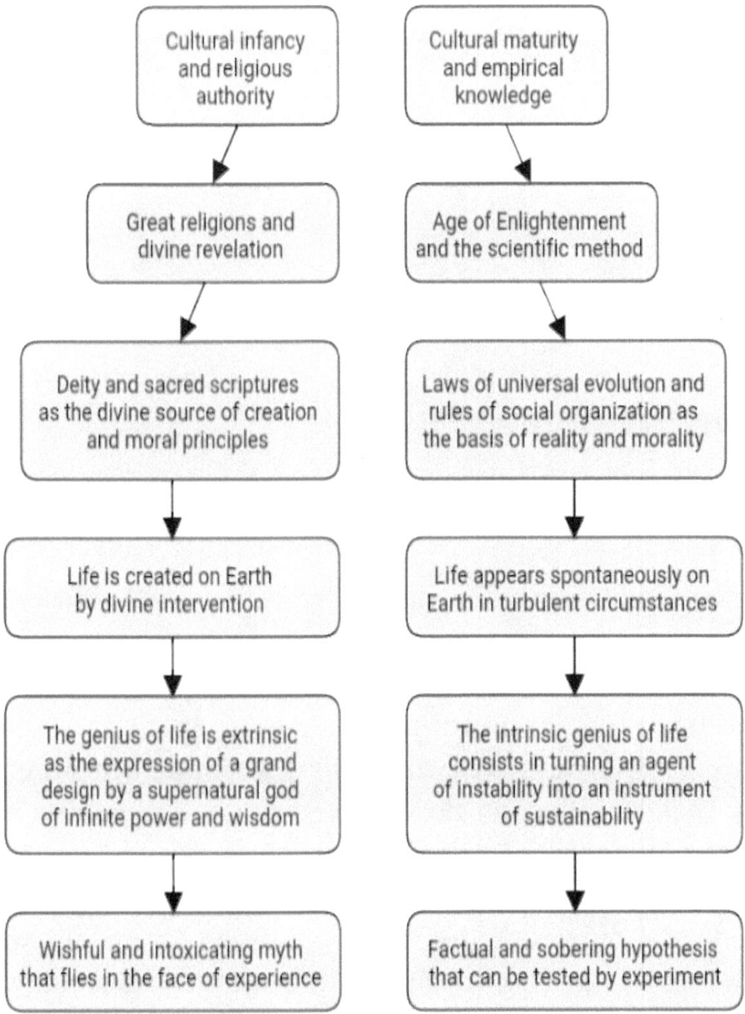

The Stranger Within

" The master of wisdom is a happy slave."

From the perspective of our conscious self, life is an everyday experiment—routinely interrupted by restorative periods of sleep—for the purpose of self-discovery and self-management. At first, we are strangers to ourselves, and only with time, observation, study, and reflection do we increasingly understand our nature, namely the complex logic and profound meaning of the interaction between us and the external world. This understanding is the necessary condition for making wise choices that are appropriate to this nature and conducive to happiness.

Now, while our consciousness is the seat of our free will where we choose the direction of our thoughts and actions, it is contingent on an autonomous and subconscious array of psychological and physiological processes that constitute the mechanical underpinnings of our experience. So the way we lead our life is equally a matter of rational deliberation, decision, and execution that fills us with assurance and dignity when successful and honorable, and a product of programmed automation that calls for trust, gratitude, and humility, like the answers to a query in a search engine, which follows advanced algorithms we did not devise, or the movements of a robot, whose sophisticated workings we did not design.

As for the external world that interacts with us and represents a vital extension of our being, it is structured by natural laws and social rules that are beyond our control, even though they may be under our influence. Above all, freedom is about accepting or refusing the shackles of unchangeable conditions (in contrast to changeable ones that we should strive to improve if they leave something to be desired). And since refusing these shackles amounts to suicide or a miserable life, which are without a doubt pitiful outcomes, accepting them is the only sensible option, pregnant with the possibility of peace and joy. The master of wisdom is a happy slave.

The Chinese have a long history of insightful philosophies, particularly Taoism and Confucianism, which advocate the peaceful and joyful acceptance of natural laws and social rules to achieve the highest standards of harmony with nature and virtue in society. We would be well advised to embrace this spirit of acceptance while exercising our critical thinking toward perverse forms of naturalness and sociability that have lapsed imprudently and complacently into laxness and servility.

True naturalness is mindfully and faithfully consistent with the creative and nurturing force that not only animates us but also gives form and function to all things in the universe. It adapts resourcefully to its surroundings and interacts lovingly with them, thereby testifying to its creative and nurturing disposition in the image of the force from which it proceeds.

Always authentic and graceful, never contrived nor labored, even when attending to difficult undertakings, true naturalness is fluent like the dance of an accomplished ballerina; it advances through life with an open mind and a kind heart, cautiously yet fearlessly, without standing in its own way. This attitude has profound relevance to the extent that our world is forever changing and challenging us to follow suit, and for the reason that everything shares the same universal essence and partakes in the same interconnected fate.

Right sociability is in line with the said attitude. It is flexible and caring, yet indignant at mediocrity or wickedness and intolerant of them, as they epitomize the worst of humanity. It sees the potential for betterment and worthiness in people, and readily provides encouragement and support toward the realization of this potential. In other words, it practices tough love where disapproval is due, instead of condoning what is reprehensible with hypocritical or complicit nods and smiles that stink of selfishness and deceit or laziness and neglect.

Summary of The Stranger Within:

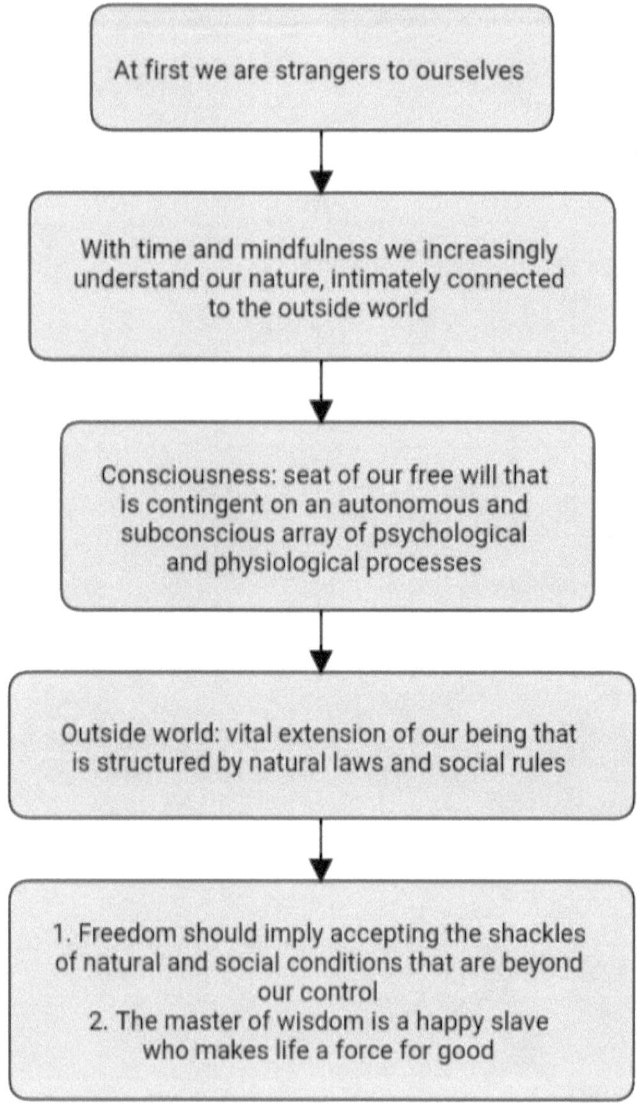

The Loss of Innocence

"For the most part our behavior is learned: It proceeds from experimentation by trial and error, and education through examples and lessons."

Among ideologies, the Genesis in the Bible and the Darwinian theory of evolution are polar opposites. And yet, at the beginning of the Genesis, the story of Adam and Eve resonates profoundly with our modern understanding of the human phenomenon in the evolution of species, if only in an allegorical sense.

The proverbial bite into the forbidden fruit from the tree of knowledge symbolizes a watershed in the history of life on Earth, as humans form a distinct evolutionary branch characterized by the loss of innocence, that is, of mindless instinctive behavior hardwired in the brain according to the genetic code.

In truth, other evolved animals share this characteristic to some limited extent, while humans are in a class of their own. Likewise, some basic human instincts remain, but for the most part our behavior is learned: It proceeds from experimentation by trial and error, and education through examples and lessons. A sense of what is good and what is bad follows, or what is efficient, healthy, gratifying, or honorable (right, in the context of our community and environment where everyone and everything is interdependent) and what is not so.

In alignment with our basic instincts, some have argued that our brain doesn't furnish us with a clean slate for the acquisition of language and knowledge. Noam Chomsky talks about a generative grammar, and Immanuel Kant, about the categories of understanding, as the innate groundwork that is laid at an early stage of development to make this acquisition possible or more easily accessible. Be that as it may, the fact that our behavior is predominantly learned (versus instinctive and genetically hardwired in the brain) remains unchallenged.

The thing is, how did we become such a distinct species? According to Stephen Jay Gould, among other evolutionary theorists, neoteny—or the retention of juvenile traits during adulthood—is the prime underlying cause that effected the quantum leap from apes to hominids. Neoteny implies some "neotenous genes" whose special function, after birth, is to impede the maturation of the human brain so that the latter keeps growing while retaining its plasticity: the prerequisite for the ability to learn. This permits a dynamic process of neuronal mapping that is informed by circumstances and can change with them time and again, resulting in new patterns of thinking or acting. This contrasts sharply with neuronal maps that are genetically determined and correspond to fixed patterns of instinctive behavior. Brain plasticity thus confers upon humans a remarkable capacity for adaptation that increases their chances of survival, whatever the situation.

It comes, however, at the expense of three primal qualities: simplicity, purity, and spontaneity. Human consciousness is often tangled—riddled with confusion and doubt or regret and shame—and labored. Only after decades of exploring and deciphering our nature, together with a firm resolution to act in accordance with this nature, can we hope to recapture those primal qualities, albeit imperfectly.

Consider the artful performance of a seasoned virtuoso, playing his instrument with a heavenly grace that appears as effortless as the warbles of a bird. Still, thousands of toilsome practice hours gradually set the stage for this performance: humble antecedent that was at first dreadfully inept, then hardly passable before becoming pleasantly decent and, at long last, masterly and worthy of praise.

Likewise, consider the enlightened way of an old monk who mindfully goes about his daily routine with utmost naturalness and calmness, in a spirit of devotion, eating or drinking measuredly if he feels hungry or thirsty, working earnestly or sitting contemplatively if he thinks it fitting to do so, and a host of other activities that follow from his vital necessities or his social and environmental responsibilities, when he is not candidly indulging in some harmless futilities. But his simple, pure, and spontaneous way was a long time coming. It arrived after a period of relative darkness spanning a good part of his life where he fumbled and faltered, slowly learning to tend the garden of his inner life for the opening of his eyes behind his eyes, the blossoming of his mind rooted in mystery. What joy and awe now fill his loving heart as he revels in the light of wisdom for some glorious years before his passing!

Summary of The Loss of Innocence:

Happiness

"Life is by definition a dynamic state that presupposes a continuous tension between needs or desires and their satisfaction."

There is a common belief that happiness amounts to the fulfillment of our needs and desires thanks to effective strategies in favorable circumstances. Is that belief truly warranted, as though anything short of the ideal it stands for translated into unhappiness or a state of mind that may include moments of joy but remains nevertheless unsatisfactory? In that case, happiness would be like water that becomes undrinkable or unpalatable when tainted.

Actually, the happiness that sages talk about is largely independent of their situation and mostly contingent on their attitude. It is a feeling of serenity that testifies to their acceptance of reality and to their clear conscience as well-adjusted and fully committed servants of life, of humanity, of nature, but above all of the divine principle that governs the universe, defined in the framework of a religious or philosophical persuasion.

While sages are aware of the subjectiveness—i.e., the individual limitations and hence the imperfection—of their outlook, they still abide by it with utmost faithfulness, if also with a willingness to correct it when they realize they have been mistaken. Their wisdom is a work in progress; it is always laced with some form of foolishness, which leaves them open to ridicule. Humility and compassion plus humor are therefore qualities that they cultivate. They mock and forgive themselves without complacency, always striving to elevate their humanness to the highest possible level of truth and moral excellence.

In summary, the secret of their happiness is a combination of surrender and struggle in response to unchangeable conditions that may be adverse or honorable goals that may be arduous. Admittedly, this is a recipe for a stern manner of joy that fills the mind rather than the heart.

It follows that this happiness leaves something to be desired: happiness in the fullest sense of the word (a state of fulfillment when everything is going our way in terms of results as well as intentions and efforts), which is a joy ever so sweet that fills both the mind and the heart.

When sages experience this supreme happiness, they rightly feel blessed and know how precarious it is.

Furthermore, they accept this precariousness or the fact that suffering and ultimately death loom ahead. Only battles are won in the fight for life that will inexorably, despite every valiant effort to prevail, end in defeat.

Some will say that happiness in its so-called fullest sense still leaves us wanting more: the power to make this happiness infinite in scope and duration. Among them, some will choose the path of faith, which allegedly leads to a heavenly afterlife, whereas some will choose the path of reason, which admits of no rosy belief based on wishful thinking and blind trust. This second path leads nowhere as far as the beyond is concerned, or rather somewhere that is unknown—presumably so different from what is known that it totally exceeds our ability to conceive of its nature.

For these proponents of reason, these "infidels," the source of meaning is not a paradisiac destination whose existence is supported by no credible evidence; it is the journey itself, a rugged and uphill journey to be sure, with an abundance of twists and turns, some of which are propitious, others not. In their eyes, this journey is well worth the trouble, independently of the paradisiac destination just mentioned. It is all about the dignity of living and loving, and the joy of succeeding in these difficult assignments to the best of their ability.

The limits imposed upon worldly happiness may initially stick in our craw, but after due consideration, as we realize that life without these limits would be death, we accept them, and better yet, we welcome them. Life is by definition a dynamic state that presupposes a continuous tension between needs or desires and their satisfaction. Render this satisfaction absolute, you resolve this tension and consequently reduce life to nothing, that is, something as inert as a stone. And this nothing—this inert something—is indeed death. Not a brilliant prospect for a life lover.

Summary of Happiness:

Happiness

In the restricted sense it is an enduring peace of mind when we surrender to immutable conditions and struggle to embody the best of humanity

In the fullest sense it is a precarious state of contentment when everything is going our way in terms of results as well as intentions and efforts

1. In the absolute sense it is infinite in scope and duration or takes the form of a heavenly afterlife that is an article of faith among religious people
2. In the minds of nonbelievers this paradisiac destination is neither credible nor sensible and the source of meaning is nowhere else than in the journey of life for better or for worse until death

The Middle Way

"The realm of existence may be regarded as the opportunity for the realm of essence to realize its potential and become self-aware."

The bonds of desire betray a state of servitude doomed to toil and turmoil, and likewise reveal a chance to experience the freedom to live and love life. This paradox spontaneously inspires us with ambivalence, which calls for a middle way between extreme detachment toward the objects of our desires and excessive attachment to them. The one is disproportionate relative to the precarious nature of life that entails the risk of suffering and the certainty of death, but also affords the possibility of fleeting joys and abiding peace; the other is immoderate, given the need to restrain our propensity for clinging to desirable things that are always subject to change.

Our human desirous self, however ephemeral, is not illusory by contrast with the divine eternal self at the heart of everything; it is equally real and must be cherished in all its transient beauty without hankering after the impossible. What is more, this human desirous self belongs to the realm of existence that manifests and thereby complements the realm of essence. Without this former realm, the latter would amount to a mere potentiality that, worse than questionable, is impossible to test and question, and is therefore naught until proven otherwise. For that reason, the realm of existence may be regarded as the opportunity for the realm of essence to realize its potential and become self-aware. It is the realm of experience and meaning.

Our first responsibility as humans is to be mindful of this experience—perceptions, emotions, reflections, and actions—in all matters to acquaint ourselves with every aspect of our complex nature, including our intimate relationship with the outside world. In doing so, we grow increasingly conscious of our three unified levels of being, which are also unified levels of becoming in the ever-changing present that constitutes the passage of time.

First level of being: It is the most immediately apparent of the three, made of habitual patterns of thought and behavior that were developed in the context of our social and natural environment. There, we are exposed daily to various sources of information and different types of situation.

Every so often, changes in that environment (e.g., disquieting but reliable information that something deemed good is in fact not so, or a troublesome and unavoidable situation that renders a certain way of acting no longer possible) challenge these habitual patterns enough to warrant their revision because they are suddenly at odds with reality and hence fail to meet the basic requirements of truth or efficiency for our survival and happiness. It then behooves us to resist the temptation of denial or renounce the familiarity of past habits to make the necessary adjustments, appropriate to the present. In short, we are challenged to adapt, on pain of dying or making our own misery.

Second level of being: This level refers to our human potential for adaptability, which normally exceeds our assumptions about it by an incredibly wide margin. When comes the time to devise suitable habits of thought or behavior in response to changes in our environment, the most reasonable attitude is a leap of faith with some measure of caution, no matter how diffident we may feel. Patience and persistence are then of the essence to find a new way of seeing or doing things and prove to ourselves that we are indeed far more resourceful than we had reckoned at the outset.

Third level of being: We reach therein the last innermost frontier of our existence, which is also the intrinsic creative matrix of everything in the universe. This matrix transcends individual deaths and can rightfully be called divine.

Science has often sought to trivialize this originative force by breaking it down into commonplace principles of organization and evolution. Truth is, there is nothing trivial about the eternal source of creation whose many distinguishable features should not distract us from its fundamental unity. No disjointed medley of forces could ever produce a human being, comprising every aspect of the universe and functioning as a unified if manifold whole. And so the proper stance toward the eternal source of creation—that can be ascertained but never explained—is humble reverence.

Summary of The Middle Way:

The paradox of life that includes both a risk of suffering and a chance of happiness calls for a middle way between extreme detachment and excessive attachment

↓

1. Our human desirous self belongs to the realm of existence that manifests and thereby complements the realm of essence
2. It is the realm of experience and meaning

↓

Our first responsibility as humans is to be mindful of this experience in order to grow increasingly conscious of our three unified levels of being:
a) habitual patterns of thought and behavior
b) human potential for adaptability
c) intrinsic creative matrix of everything in the universe

The Field of Things

"The natural order would blend necessity and randomness, in the image of improvisational jazz that loosely follows a melody."

Despite the best efforts of scientists and philosophers, the question of universal determinism is beyond theoretical certainty, as no amount of knowledge will ever exhaust the full measure of this question, ranging from the infinitely small to the infinitely large and extending through time infinitely.

Mind you, there is not a single human theory that is exempt from this imperfection for the selfsame reason. Does this reduce the scientific and philosophical enterprise to a pointless exercise? Assuredly not, as it is a useful means of inhabiting the world meaningfully if in part fancifully. Every general truth that attempts to make sense of the intricate workings of the universe is therefore always presumptive and tentative, open to doubt; it is both subject to corroboration and liable to revision or refutation.

Having said this, one theory of universal determinism seems particularly compelling, all the more as it rings intuitively true. Neither strictly deterministic nor totally indeterministic, this theory is probabilistic to a variable extent, not merely for the sake of operational convenience because of limitations in the process of measurement, but more fundamentally as an expression of the natural order. The latter would blend necessity and randomness, in the image of improvisational jazz that loosely follows a melody (an excellent metaphor that belongs to the astrophysicist Hubert Reeves). It would thus take the shape of a field that is determined as a circumscribed whole governed by laws, but undetermined within its circumscription where anything goes.

A familiar example is the determination to buy an apple, mixed with the indetermination regarding what apple we will choose in a heap of comparably palatable apples, leaving the act of choosing to arbitrariness. By the same token, at the microscopic level, the behavior of elementary particles would be indeterminate within a circumscribed field of possibilities, whereas the field itself would have a determinate circumscription. Only large numbers of these particles considered as an organized mass would behave in a strictly deterministic way, like a billiard ball that has collided with another. Similarly, a multitude of individuals intent on buying an apple would collectively and predictably buy all the apples in a given heap.

Another example, which comes from *The Structure of Scientific Revolutions* by Thomas Kuhn, is worthy of note: "Although observation and experience drastically restrict the range of admissible scientific belief, they cannot alone determine a particular body of such belief." The restricted range in question may be construed as a circumscribed field of theoretical thinking wherein a number of different theories that agree with facts can be conceived. In other words, empirical evidence allows for a certain degree of liberty in devising a theoretical framework that accounts for it.

To sum up, the appearance of strict determinism at the macroscopic level of common observation points to an epistemic problem, having to do with the conditions of knowledge, not an ontological one, having to do with the nature of being. Accordingly, if we increase the granularity of observation to the quantum level, we enter a subatomic microcosm in which straight lines gain considerable breadth and become fields where the passage from A to B offers multiple possibilities.

This type of latitude within a circumscribed field of available options could be dubbed "the freedom of redundancy" where determinacy, characterized by rigid uniformity, is tempered with indeterminacy, bringing flexibility and variability into the fold. It would constitute a margin of tolerance that preserves the effectiveness of an action, notwithstanding variations in execution, as long as this margin is not exceeded and these variations remain insignificant for all intents and purposes. As such, it would be beneficial, just as a buffer in a business or financial activity can protect it against the shock of fluctuations.

In addition to the freedom of redundancy, a second type of freedom exists that is specific to humans and presumably—but to a lesser extent—other intelligent mammals like chimpanzees and dolphins. Let us call it "the freedom of consciousness."

In the case of humans, consciousness is a sophisticated display of perceptions, emotions, recollections, inventions, and cogitations that introduces a new dimension in the field of determinism. Behavior is no longer the product of a purely automatic process but of a conscious choice, interlaced with subconscious impulses. In everything we accomplish freely and deliberately, the prime force at work is the decision to act in accordance with some aesthetic, hedonistic, hygienic, ethical, logical, or otherwise rational standard. This decision can be weakened by confusion and faintheartedness, and lead to vacillation, or prove articulate and mettlesome, and be conducive to firm action. It therefore stands to reason that clear-mindedness and resolve are the sine qua non for effective self-determination. Barring that, the freedom of consciousness is a shameful mess of hazy notions and wavering intentions that leave a lot to be desired.

Summary of The Field of Things:

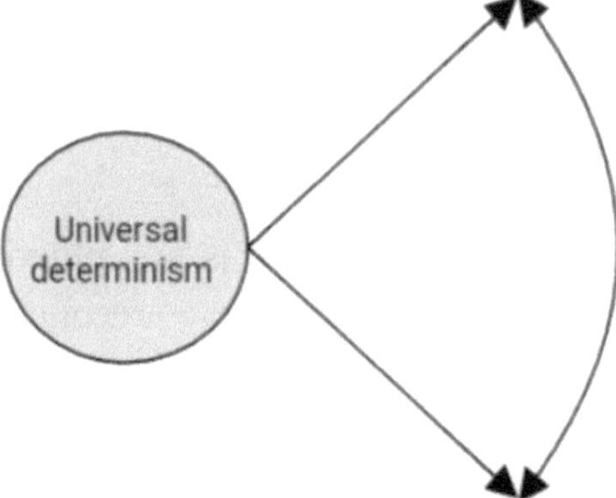

God and Divine Love Revisited

"Perhaps the most balanced, comprehensive, and truthful approach lies in philosophy, at the crossroads between religious and scientific traditions."

According to Stephen Hawking, "Mysticism is for those who can't do the math." While this man's repute as a brilliant physicist cannot legitimately be challenged, should we not question his antireligious quip, which may betray, his brilliance notwithstanding, the failure of his reason to validate the profound insights of the heart (the locus of our subjective experience in the form of affects, by contrast with their behavioral effects) beyond the confines of hard science or materialistic objectivity?

Surely, the validation of these insights should not be done wholesale without critical thinking. Throughout the ages, prominent mystics from a variety of cultural backgrounds have founded religions that not only bear the stamp of their spiritual knowledge but also of the ignorance, delusions, and questionable conventions of their time.

A champion of atheism like Richard Dawkins has the merit of subjecting these religions to a rigorous analysis, based on scientific evidence, which serves as a litmus test to determine whether a belief is credible. Having said this, his stance and that of comparable detractors should be taken with a grain of salt. Science has its strengths and limitations, pertaining to its outward focus and rational method of inquiry.

Perhaps the most balanced, comprehensive, and truthful approach lies in philosophy (including epistemology, logic, metaphysics, and ethics), at the crossroads between religious and scientific traditions. This approach would advocate a courageous and respectful disposition to acknowledge or investigate new facts and new ideas in a spirit of tolerance and integrity. It would also demand empirical and methodological rigor in defining and processing evidence, while remaining vigilant and adamant against the most patently and offensively inane or insane persuasions. No tolerance can be absolute without welcoming its opposite and destroying itself, thereby setting the stage for anarchy where the highest values of civilization—liberty, equality, and fraternity—no longer rule and might is right.

Now, beyond the many points of contention that pit great religions (Hinduism, Judaism, Christianity, and Islam) against one another and other belief systems, all the more divisively as they each claim (in some Vedas, the Torah, the Bible, and the Quran) to be divinely inspired and absolutely true, what fundamental notions can generate consensus among the followers of these religions and likewise can survive the scrutiny of philosophers, who dare listen to the voice of experience and think for themselves?

Let us consider two such notions in their most generic and least contentious acceptation: God, as the creative force at the heart of creation, and divine love, as the gift of existence and resilience that "God" bestows unreservedly upon everything it creates.

Defined in these terms, "God" is compatible with science, which details the many ways it manifests itself through time and space in the form of physical forces, as opposed to nonphysical ones that elude science (its methodology focuses exclusively on spatiotemporal phenomena, which are observable, accountable, and predictable). Together these physical and nonphysical forces can be subsumed under the single, albeit multifaceted, nature of "God" because they drive the creation of complex yet unified entities—the most telling example being us humans at the top of the evolutionary pyramid.

As for divine love, it is an eloquent metaphor inspired by motherly love to describe the nurturing aspect of "God," manifested via the gift of existence and resilience. "God" is here a core metaphysical concept representing the prime cause of everything. As such, it is somewhat of a misnomer because it departs from its anthropomorphic acceptation found in the sacred texts of great religions.

For that reason, we shall simply refer to it as the creative and nurturing force at the heart of creation.

A burning question remains: If the nurturing aspect of this creative force is reminiscent of motherly love, insofar as a mother gives birth to a child and promotes its well-being to the best of her ability, does the similitude extend to the limited nature of this ability (the limitations explain why a mother, despite her best intentions, can fail to safeguard her child against all manner of ills)? If the answer is yes, then the so-called almightiness of God, as portrayed by the founding mystics of great religions, is a myth indicative of wishful thinking. In other words, the power of the creative and nurturing force at the heart of creation is immense but not unlimited, and the possibility of suffering and death is an understandable and unavoidable consequence of this sobering fact.

Summary of God and Divine Love Revisited:

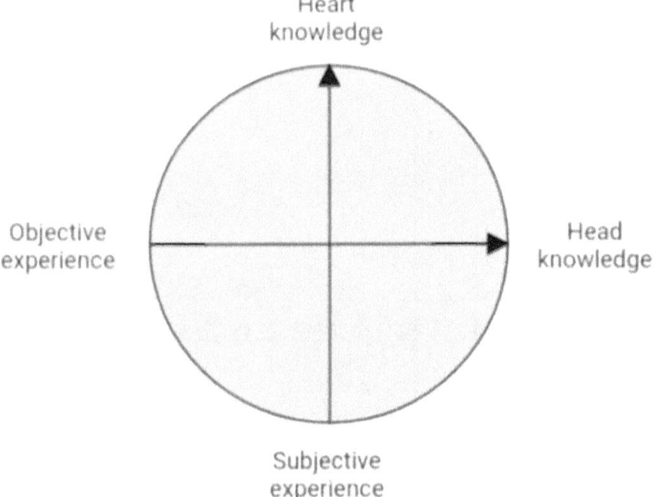

The Spectrum of Life and Love

"Life is the biological art of turning a bad situation to good account."

The highest level of awareness is our communion with the creative and nurturing force at the heart of creation and ipso facto at the heart of humans: personal incarnations of this force in time and space. We are one with yet distinct from the transpersonal, timeless, and ubiquitous force itself, which is concurrently nowhere—as a transcendent, immutable, and unmanifested potential—and everywhere—as a worldly, evolutionary, and manifested potential. Evolution comprises a threefold dimension of time in the form of past (what is no longer extant), present (what is extant), and future (what is not yet extant). Put differently, it implies a forever-changing present with a perpetual alternation of potentiality and actuality.

The highest level of realization is our embodiment of the creative and nurturing force at the heart of creation. It is both enabled and restricted by our incarnate human nature, which doesn't share the universal and eternal scope of this force.

Of course we can transcend our human—local and mortal—condition through identification with our divine—universal and eternal—foundation; but in the event that we take this identification to an extreme of asceticism, it would entail a renunciation of our human condition. And that would undoubtedly be premature, as we are called to actualize the potential specific to this condition in the most authentic and fulfilling way until we are clearly spent and about to draw our last breath.

Let us explore the creative aspect of the force at the heart of creation and ipso facto at the heart of humans. The process of creation gravitates toward predetermined attractors along two main evolutionary lines: inert things and living beings.

Inert things reach their maximum resistance in the form of hard solids that can withstand external forces (mechanical, thermal, or other) while maintaining the stability and integrity of their inert structure. In the form of gases or watery liquids, inert things are most precarious, and these external forces subject them to disturbances that may be regarded as transitional toward entropy. The latter can only be attained when all thermodynamic differences between these things and their surroundings have leveled off.

As for living beings, they stand everything on its head. The formerly unstabilizing effect of external forces on fluid physical systems is converted into an agent of stabilization that allows living beings to maintain the integrity of their dynamic structure through constant regeneration. It is as though life was originally a state of disturbance that had fully embraced its negentropic nature (far from entropy or thermodynamic equilibrium) into a sort of dissipative system that takes energy in its environment as a means of sustenance.

In brief, life is the biological art of turning a bad situation to good account. And it seems appropriate for us to mimic this remarkable trait of our constitution in our attitude and behavior by remaining positive and adaptable in all circumstances, while entertaining a realistic outlook that portrays things as they are—always liable to change.

Let us now explore the nurturing aspect of the force at the heart of creation, especially as regards living beings. To acquaint ourselves intimately with this aspect, we ought to look deep into the gift of life, which includes the capacity to endure and overcome hardships, and even thrive, albeit within limits that imply the risk of baleful outcomes. This gift is above all a divine bounty that evokes an act of motherly love. Clearly, this is a metaphorical representation. It is nonetheless profoundly insightful and meaningful.

In the end, there is nothing more authentic and fulfilling than, on the one hand, to develop a positive and adaptable temperament, and on the other hand, to dedicate our life to the labor of love, beginning with self-love and expanding it—through a sense of social and environmental belonging, and through mystical identification with our higher self—to the love of everyone and everything, inasmuch as we can conciliate this expanded kindness with the one we owe to ourselves. We are after all the vital starting point of this inward journey.

Summary of The Spectrum of Life and Love:

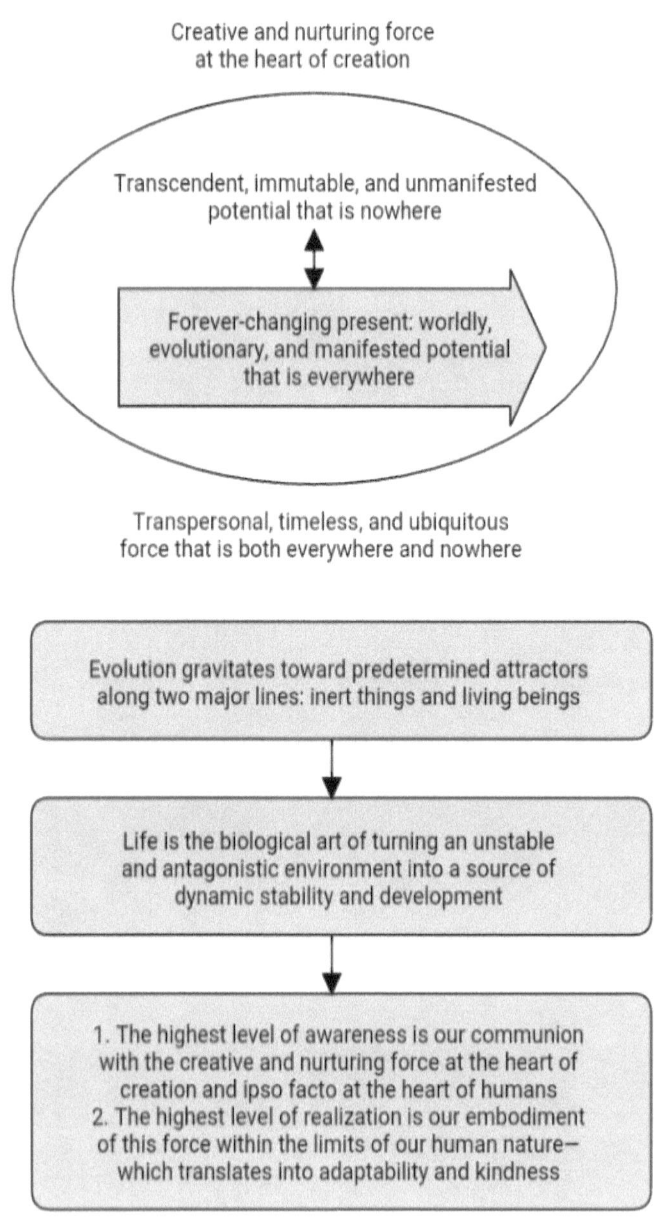

The Emotional Minefield

"The combination of consciousness and intelligence can only operate effectively and generate favorable outcomes when the mind is calm."

The emotional core of a human being is a potential liability. Beyond a critical threshold of intensity, emotions can dominate our field of consciousness and defeat our ability to view things clearly and realistically.

Take for example a positive and rapturous emotion like love at first sight; it is blind to the faults of an alluring stranger and may lead to romance that ends in breakup once reality sets in. Negative emotions are even more treacherous and worrisome. Anger and hate can run amok and leave in their wake more grief and shame than the heart can bear.

It is as if the inner landscape of our consciousness was a hazardous minefield. Each mine represents an emotional trigger, and we must devise a strategy to avoid unleashing their explosive potential or at least contain it within manageable bounds that allow our reason to function unhampered and prove congruent with our individual, social, and environmental purpose, both short-term and long-term.

As a priority, we ought to extricate ourselves regularly from the daily hustle and bustle to reflect on every aspect of our life with focus and composure. We then improve our self-knowledge as part of a multiple but interconnected and unified whole that is ever-changing.

With time, our reflective practice becomes second-nature and goes on to include every awakened moment of our existence in a continuum of revealing awareness. This practice is instrumental in clearly defining the inner circle of the people and things that matter most to us and compel our dedication. The same can be said of the principles and values that we deem worthy above every other and hence follow with the steadfast adherence of the enlightened. The latter bring out the best in their human nature and serve as role models who inspire others to better themselves.

Again, it must be stressed that the combination of consciousness and intelligence—as the source of self-knowledge and self-direction through observation and reflection—can only operate effectively and generate favorable outcomes when the mind is calm: free from extreme emotional disturbances. Consequently, our chief mental imperative is to be on the lookout for these disturbances.

More precisely, we must forbear saying or doing reckless things when we go haywire with anger, fear, disgust, hate, or any other negative emotion that can prompt a perverse reaction, by contrast with a sound course of action that is constructive, not counterproductive or downright destructive. To that effect, we would be well advised to call a timeout, breathe deeply, and take a step back from the circumstances that triggered an emotional storm. We can then put things into perspective, as we calm ourselves down. If however this is not feasible, we may end up with no better option than to do damage control with apologies and other balms at our disposal.

Perhaps the optimal scenario is to enjoy a ready-made bulwark against such a derailment and its aftermath. The key is to cultivate a wise outlook, as it holds aspirations and expectations that are appropriate to our reality and therefore unlikely to spawn tumultuous feelings of absolute antagonism or utter letdown.

Of course—and legitimately so—we may still experience negative emotions like anger, fear, disgust, and hate toward certain situations that are painfully at odds with our pursuit of fairness, safety, dignity, kindness, and other desirables that are conducive to happiness. The difference, however, will be significant insofar as our wise outlook provides the framework for these emotions and spontaneously tempers them with a general attitude of compassion, gumption, humility, and cordiality, among other signs of a favorable disposition. This attitude bodes well for us and the world around us, which together form a network of beings and things that exist in a state of universal linkage and kinship.

Consider the unsavory opposite: a bad emotional rut that derives from a jaundiced mindset (e.g., people are evil; we are worthless; life is all gloom and doom; the odds are stacked against us, and other aberrations that err on the side of pessimism and defeatism), which induces us to perceive every situation in the same dreary hue as through a dark filter. We must be wary of these toxic mental states and defy them with critical thinking in order to defuse them. This is all the more important as such toxic mental states lead to adverse behaviors that can wreak havoc with our life in the worst way.

All in all, whatever emotion fills our heart, whether it be negative or positive, we had better wait for our reason to find its footing and strike a balance between hot-blooded feeling and cool-headed thinking. The object of this constraint is to keep from acting wildly and blindly, without reviewing the full gamut of our wants and duties, and without weighing the pros and cons, thereby dangerously augmenting the risk of a pathetic or ignominious setback. Indeed, who in their right mind would relish such an outcome, which clashes sorely with their inborn predilection for harmony and happiness in every part of life?

Summary of The Emotional Minefield:

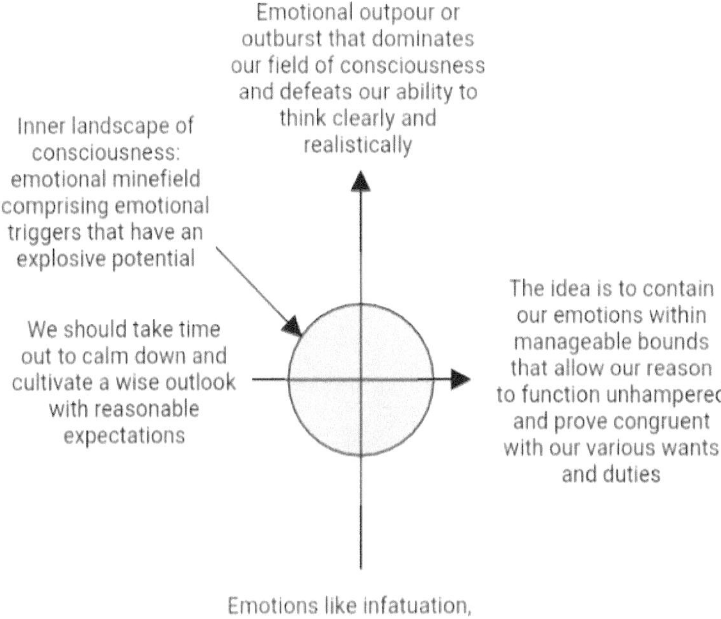

The Puzzle of Life

"We are reliant on nature and society, and the multiplicity of interactions between us and them are integral to our reality."

We live in what is typically referred to as the age of information. Regrettably, this age is often appropriated by individuals and groups that are either unprincipled and manipulative or unwise and fanatical, and pervert it into a self-serving or self-indulgent age of fabrications and delusions. What is more, this hodgepodge of sense and nonsense is so miscellaneous and humongous that many of us feel overwhelmed and riffle through it confusedly, just enough to know a smattering of everything, including all manner of falsehoods and half-truths. We then lapse into the category of scattered brains that lack focus and depth, and whose only merit is to pass for entertaining conversationalists.

Think of the difference between such scattered brains—responding with indiscriminate and superficial curiosity to a variety of stimuli from the outside world—and animals that are hardwired to act instinctively. These animals have a single-minded objective: to survive and reproduce, to extend their survival beyond the scope of their individual lives. Hence, whatever piques their interest or motivates their behavior relates essentially to a vital goal from which they never stray. This gives them a grounded quality of sorts that is profoundly lacking in people who have lost their compass in the midst of agitation, distraction, confusion, and often dejection.

The critical question is how to develop this grounded quality in a distinctively human way that harnesses our twofold potential of experience and intelligence toward self-awareness and self-realization. The answer consists in a mindful presence to every aspect of our existence from the moment we wake up to the moment we go to sleep. With time, two things become glaringly obvious.

1) We are a combination of life (the torso, which contains the vital organs) and physical or mental tools (the limbs and the head) whose purpose is to make life possible through appropriate exertions that show a strong will, together with good judgment in the assessment of obstacles and opportunities. These exertions are self-promoting inasmuch as they help us thrive, and this self-promotion amounts to self-love. It is redolent of the nurturing attention that a mother lavishes on her child.

2) We are embedded in our natural and social environment, and form with it an interconnected whole that extends to the entire universe. Of course, on the surface, our self appears to be separate from this environment, but a deeper inquiry provides evidence to the contrary. We are reliant on nature and society, and the multiplicity of interactions between us and them are integral to our reality. In other words, our self is an empty concept if we abstract it from everything—either proximate or distant—that is linked to it intimately. It is individual by nature and universal by extension. This logically implies that our self-love should be infinitely inclusive and lead to an unrestricted promotion of life within and without, or at least as comprehensive and benevolent as our human constitution and character permit.

Bearing in mind these two things, let us picture our time on Earth as a jigsaw puzzle that displays an image of individual life and universal love. Also let us picture all the things we do or say as the pieces of this puzzle that fit together to compose that image and thus represent the diverse manifestations of our general purpose: to live and to love. Only when these diverse manifestations are mindfully infused with that purpose can we consider ourselves truly self-aware and self-realized as exemplars of fortitude, liveliness, gratitude, kindness, and a host of other qualities that crown the business of living and loving.

Summary of The Puzzle of Life:

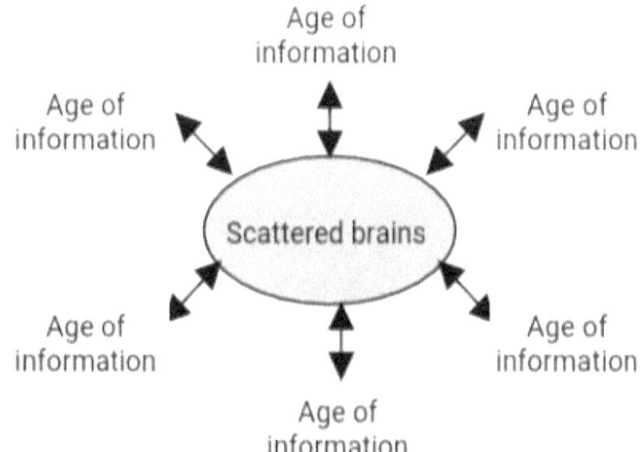

Overwhelming hodgepodge of sense and nonsense
that is often a source of distraction and confusion
that alienates us from ourselves

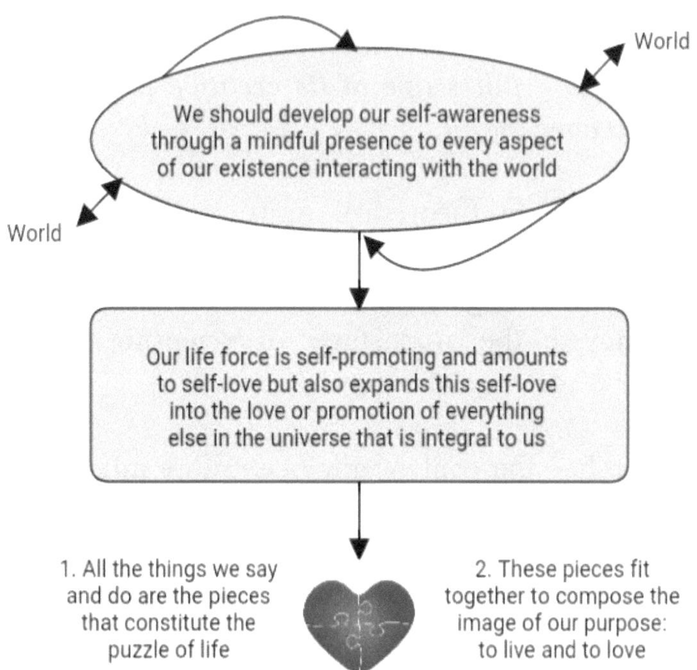

The Cosmic Striptease

"The creative principle at the core of everything never manifests the full scope of its creative potential all at once and once for all."

For the sake of theoretical unity and parsimony, the attempted reduction of special sciences (e.g., biology) and social sciences (e.g., psychology) to fundamental physics has enjoyed the mainstage of scientific orthodoxy, however controversial it may be.

Nowhere has the controversy been more intense than in the attempted reduction of psychology to neuroscience, in the first instance, and ultimately to fundamental physics. Other social sciences have been targeted, like sociology and economics, to no avail. Why? Is the failure contingent on current scientific limitations or is it inevitable regardless of progress in the future? That is, will it eventually be overcome with a further advancement of fundamental physics or is it to be expected indefinitely because the attempted reduction in question is by nature inappropriate to its object and unfeasible?

To begin with, how can consciousness, which is the foundation of experience and consequently of science itself, be relegated to the status of epiphenomenon as a derivative of matter that can virtually be ignored? Then again, what is matter? Who, save the most naive among us, can say in all seriousness that they have seen or felt it, when in fact nothing is ever experienced but our perceptions in our field of consciousness? These perceptions can at best be regarded as a relatively faithful representation of the outer world mediated by our inner world. Furthermore, when we describe this outer world as material, how can we not stop in our tracks with a feeling of strangeness, as its so-called concreteness or tangibleness appears on second thought incredibly abstract and intangible?

And yet, we must forbear indulging our propensity for oversimplification, whether it be reductive materialism or reductive idealism. Reality always resists either errancy with relentless insistence. With time, we must concede the point: The outer world is not a mere offshoot of our inner world, as often evidenced by its contrary character that suggests a weighty otherness, just as our inner world is not a mere spinoff of the outer world, whose concrete manifestation is empirically void without the former, in all its immateriality hinged on materiality. In short, though reality is fundamentally one, it is irreducibly twofold. It comprises a perceiving subject and a perceived object, which together constitute the subjective experience of things. Similarly, a coin is a single piece of currency but it presents two distinct faces: head and tail.

To help seal our antireductionist contention, let us make a leap of imagination. Aboard a special ship that affords time travel and provides an artificial and autonomous biosphere in which we can live safely regardless of circumstances, we return to the beginning of the universe some 14 billion years ago when all that existed was a chaotic plasma: a dense and gaseous mixture of supercharged particles subjected to extreme high temperature after the Big Bang.

The problem is, the unexpected side effect of this extraordinary voyage is irreversible amnesia, leaving us nearly as ignorant as a newborn child, were it not for the peculiar fact that we are still fluent in our native language and proficient at handling our special ship. Our curiosity is inexhaustible and our faculties, prodigious thanks to sophisticated techniques of bioengineering. We proceed forthwith to observe and strive to understand the nature of our new and alien surroundings, equipped with the most advanced tools of inquiry.

Suddenly, while getting reacquainted with our image in a mirror, a puzzling epiphany overtakes us in the form of a conundrum: How can we make sense of our existence in the context of this universal wasteland where a sweltering mess of agitated little nothings prevail in an expanse of emptiness; to wit, against all odds, by what miracle did we come to be? And when? And where? Haunted by this unanswered question, we go about our business and later go to sleep.

Upon waking up, an inkling pops into our mind, bringing some meaning to offset our puzzlement. Could it be that the universe is akin to an exotic dancer who has mastered the art of sustaining our interest by revealing only incrementally, and very slowly at that, with tantalizing poses, her toothsome nudity? To put it in less metaphorical terms, could it be that the creative principle at the core of everything never manifests the full scope of its creative potential all at once and once for all. Quite the contrary, it manifests this potential in stages, evolutionarily, with each stage (plus associated structures and functions) introducing a new opportunity for the emergence of the next stage and so on and so forth until humanity not only becomes possible but very likely.

As vaguely anticipated, space expands by force of the initial explosion, with the result that everything cools, and lo and behold a critical phase transition takes place. The little nothings become little somethings of ordinary matter, which display discernible patterns of motion. They lay the groundwork for the formation of increasingly complex bodies, inert or living, over billions of years of evolution until the welcome advent of humanity. Well, from our perspective at least.

Summary of The Cosmic Striptease:

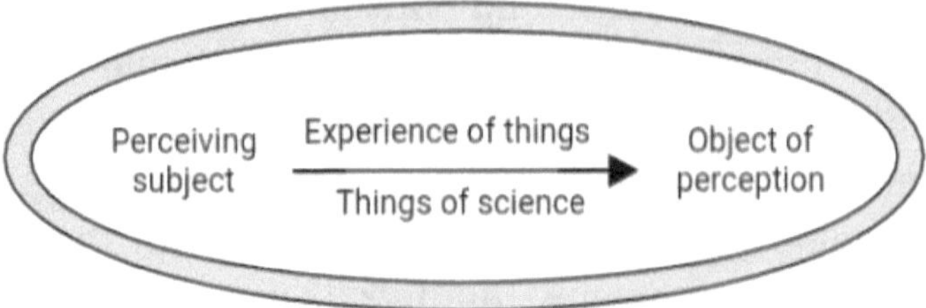

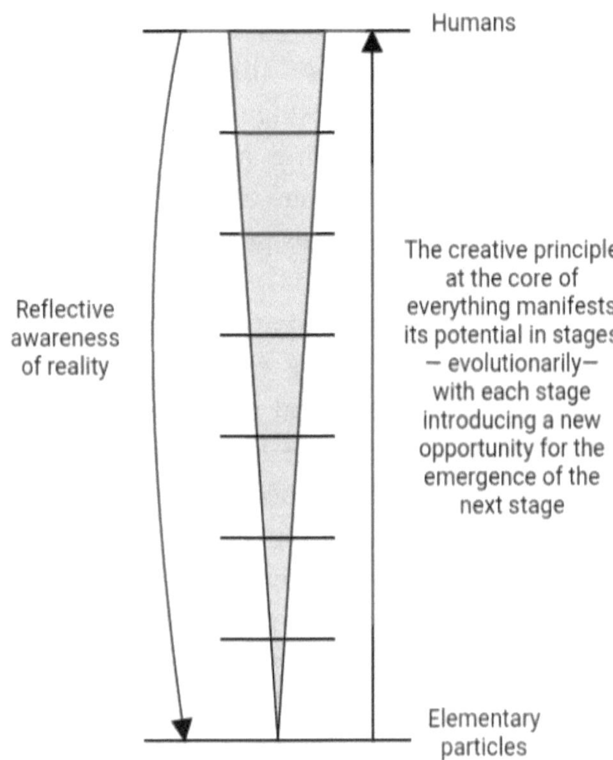

The Bright Side

"We have the gift of reason and imagination thanks to which we can generate meaning and joy from a labor of discovery, acceptance, and adaptation."

There are two main philosophical stances that can be adopted toward life: acceptance and rejection. According to the latter (typically labeled "rejectionism" or "antinatalism"), life is such a burden of suffering that it is immoral to bring a child into the world.

Counterintuitively, this philosophical stance—currently spearheaded by the South African philosopher David Benatar—has primarily taken root as an existential malaise in economically developed countries. On second thought, however, it stands to reason that people who enjoy material affluence have the leisure to ruminate on the meaning of life and sometimes arrive at a dreary conclusion, as in the present case. Incidentally, this sort of pessimism has a long history that dates back to Eastern traditions, namely Hinduism (the pursuit of Moksha: release from the cycle of death and rebirth) and Buddhism (the selfsame pursuit whose object is here called Nirvana), both based on the premise that life is a hotbed of misery.

Acceptance, on the other hand, testifies to a favorable outlook that portrays our time on Earth as worthwhile by virtue of many valuable experiences, notwithstanding impediments and hardships. Examples are serenity and dignity, from finding purpose in life and striving to achieve it, together with desirable outcomes like sensuous pleasure and intellectual gratification. Acceptance therefore hinges on a value judgment, as does its opposite but with a different conclusion and corollary determination: to procreate, which complements the resolve to live.

Whatever philosophical stance we adopt, the choice is always personal, as averred by Jean-Paul Sartre, the author of the novel Nausea where Roquentin, the protagonist, expresses strong rejectionist ideas. In fact, it is the most important choice that someone can make, both in relation to their own life and that of a possible child, as to whether life is worth the trouble and birth is in this child's best interest. Furthermore, this choice is a distinctively human aspect of our nature, in contrast to animals whose survival is entirely instinctive.

The problem with this possible child is precisely that it is not yet a person, capable of making their own decision based on experience, following some extended examination of the pros and cons of existence. But is it right to deny this child the opportunity to live and the freedom to decide one way or the other, in the name of a sinister and controversial ideology that belongs to a minority group of questionable sanity and wisdom?

It appears safe to suggest that "no" is the correct answer to this question, especially since the assumption that we know better than others what suits them best, enough to act against their will, presently or in the future (as in the will of a future human endowed with the gift of thought), is a blamable form of totalitarian arrogance that should be dismissed out of hand.

The "no" is doubly justified as the conviction of those who advocate rejectionism is suspect, to the extent that paradoxically they find enough motivation to face the music daily and write books about the human predicament. But let's say for argument's sake that in their eyes the feeling that life is worth living is a boon they personally enjoy against a backdrop of widespread misery, implying that their joy is terribly restricted, the appanage of a privileged minority. How did they come to this view? By referring to surveys of subjective happiness worldwide? Truth is, the common perception is not that life isn't worth living.

David Benatar argues there is ample evidence that people are naturally biased toward life and overestimate the quality of their condition, thereby skewing the conclusions found in these surveys. His argument, however, is flawed on two counts: 1) statistics, however informative, are not the proper litmus test for determining whether a person has good reasons to live or procreate; and 2) this overestimation betrays a favorable disposition that is welcome in the personal assessment of one's existence, this assessment trumping any claim to the contrary.

In any event, the gloomy take on life and the related childless or suicidal cure (although many rejectionists do not endorse suicide as a method of extinction) remain suspicious as long as their proponents prefer life to death on a personal level. Cases in point, after years of literary, philosophical, or political engagement, plus reflections about rejectionism as being the ultimate expression of reason and freedom, Arthur Schopenhauer, Emil Cioran, Samuel Beckett, and Jean-Paul Sartre, among others who often portrayed life unfavorably, died of old age.

Note that Schopenhauer is among those who do not endorse suicide, but his position appears somewhat contradictory. In suicide, the basic assumption is that life is so wretched that the absence of it is a welcome relief, and one decides to act against the instinctive will to live by killing oneself. As for Schopenhauer's line of reasoning, it is similarly that life is so wretched that the absence of it is a welcome relief; hence, we should act against the instinctive will to live by denying it in a general attitude of renunciation, but only up to a point. Life is barely maintained by a strict minimum that amounts to asceticism until death. The difference between the two attitudes—suicidal on the one side and ascetic on the other—is rather a question of degree versus of nature. Either we are dead dead or dead alive, and both outcomes have nothing to do with the hardy task of living fully, no matter how vulnerable and transient life is.

In fairness to David Benatar, who sees in antinatalism a nonviolent and moral stand that prevents a child from suffering, as opposed to suicide that is a violent and selfish measure that grieves family members and friends, a distinction can be drawn between the one and the other. This distinction, however, seems more like an exercise in splitting hairs, as fundamentally they both follow from the same nihilistic premise: Non-existence is preferable to existence.

Truth is, this bleak notion is just that, a notion, and a pathetic one at that. More defensible is the reverse idea, except in extreme cases where someone's condition is hopelessly unbearable. In all other cases, studies about happiness reveal the consensus that it depends far less on circumstances than on the attitude of the individual who can or cannot integrate the various aspects of their existence into a meaningful and fulfilling whole, and as a result feels motivated to push on or not.

Thus, the contention that the procreative act sets the stage for considerable hardship is grossly incomplete without this rebuttal: The procreative act sets the stage for considerable happiness, which redeems the trouble along the way. More importantly, whether life is worth living is a grave question that can only be settled properly by the value judgment of the person involved, against which any generalization—subjective or objective, dubbed "scientific" or not—is moot.

Having said that, ancient wisdom, both Eastern and Western, teaches us that meaninglessness and unhappiness are transitional in the journey from ignorance to knowledge. Not the tendentious knowledge according to which the apex of awareness is the turning point in evolution when humans deliberately defy their existence to terminate it. As though the end game of the creative and nurturing force at the heart of the evolutionary process was the annihilation of its most accomplished incarnation! We have the gift of reason and imagination thanks to which we can generate meaning and joy from a labor of discovery, acceptance, and adaptation.

Again, the personal assessment of our life is the only apposite measurement for determining its value, even if the positive spin we put on it is regarded as a mark of bias (such is the case with Benatar and other thinkers of the same ilk who would likely paint sunshine in shades of grey) rather than wisdom.

Liberation from the cycle of misery doesn't have to take the form of avoidance, spiritual or mundane; on the contrary, it can be a more enlightened sense of engagement in the worthwhile, albeit hazardous, adventure of life. Every day is an opportunity to live and learn as we strive to be the best—most enterprising and loving—that we can be, for our own sake and that of others whose fate we share interdependently.

Life must be considered a fluid entity within an equally fluid reality where flux brings new challenges, new tensions in need of resolution. Nothing, however desirable, can be retained indefinitely any more than water can be trapped by clenching hands. Hence, life is not for the faint of heart; but for those who value and practice the virtue of courage and go the distance to minimize suffering and maximize happiness for themselves and fellow human beings (not to mention fellow living forms), a world of purpose and joy is available to them.

Change is in the nature of life, inclusive of everything good, besides everything bad; in a word, it just is, open to all perspectives, positive or negative. And while we stay cautious in light of the negative, we had better heed the positive lest we miss it like a passing train bound for contentment and gratitude. Yes, life and the things we cherish will eventually be lost, but this future loss should never spoil the present gain, renewed time and again in one form or another.

In the end, the onus is on us to ponder our human condition, day in day out, on the basis of experience. We can then develop a wise outlook that offers an insightful view of what this condition represents as a dynamic and interactive process. Likewise, we can establish priorities and use them as an inner compass.

For example, we may posit that we are an incarnate life force induced to work at surviving and thriving. We may further argue that to do so is a nurturing endeavor (not counting the fact that it is also creative in dealing with changing circumstances) best encapsulated by the concept of self-love as a visceral concern for our welfare. Finally, we may elevate this argument to the level of a moral imperative that extends our self-love to the love for all that exists, as part of our social or natural environment, which is a vital complement to our existence. We thereby transfigure our life force into a love force that translates into a staunch promotion of life within and without, including whatever contributes to its fulfillment, like health, freedom, and the power to succeed.

We may even fit this view in a metaphysical framework, so that the plurality of things and beings in the universe are subsumed under a single creative and nurturing force that accounts for their existence and resilience. Yet, notwithstanding the fundamental unity of the universe, this plurality of things and beings often conflict with one another and require an effort of resolution.

This conflict may shock us at first blush because it entails the risk of suffering as the aftermath of antagonistic actions. We may nevertheless breathe a sigh of relief at the thought of this twofold solution: ingenuity and cooperation. There is indeed formidable strength in numbers with a pooling of means united by a set of shared objectives. Our life in solidarity with others may then be seen as an organic part of a living mosaic.

The point of this thinking exercise is to turn our crude existential fact into an elaborate worldview. The outcome is an enlightened sense of purpose, like a beacon guiding our travels through the fog of our difficult existence.

Summary of The Bright Side:

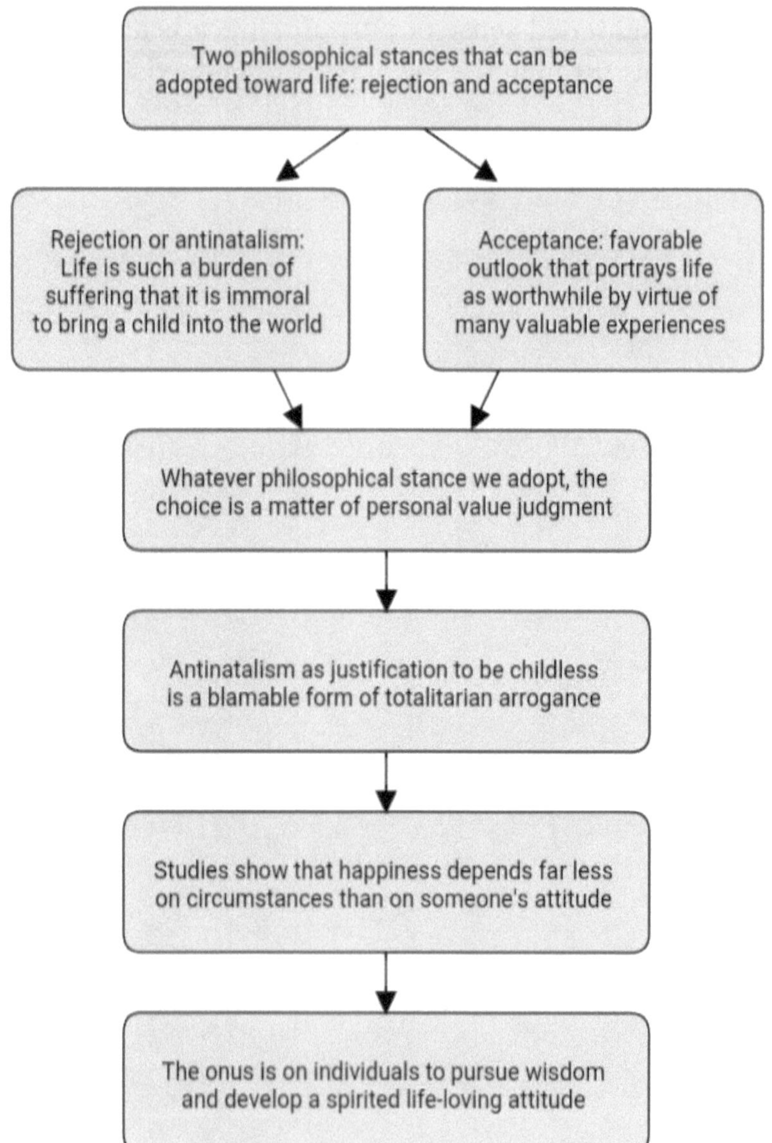

Between Life and Death

"It is not the duration of life but its quality that matters most."

Most of us are averse to talking about our eventual death, not to mention our struggles and troubles along the way before that fateful day. Life is a serious game that comes with this iron rule: You want to play, you have to pay, and the price is the obvious darkness that shadows the bright side of life inexorably, although we usually prefer to stay oblivious to it. Moreover, the question of death implies another that is also thorny and hard to handle: the question of what sort of death will befall us, short and painless or agonizingly drawn out, as in certain terminal illnesses that exclude any quality of life worth mention, beyond the mindless rote of a heartbeat.

In the latter case, would we not likely fail to see the point of such hopeless misery, as it defeats our ability to treasure the gift of days, which have morphed into a nightmarish burden? Perhaps some would find purpose in a grandstand display of misplaced heroism against the victor, namely the ailment that has laid their body to waste, save a faint ability to fight on in the most futile and pathetic way. Then again, some might choose to suffer stoically while entrusting their life to God and praying for mercy, with nothing but an extended agony to show for their prayers. Be that as it may, euthanasia would necessarily cross the mind of anyone who is subjected to such a wretched plight, as a poignantly relevant alternative.

Euthanasia has a long history that begins in ancient Greece where it was common practice despite certain thinkers opposing it for religious or philosophical reasons. Its intent was "a good death:" a peaceful and voluntary passing under controlled circumstances to end suffering, particularly during a terminal illness, thereby avoiding a prolonged state of extreme and irreversible affliction that was deemed pointless.

With the appropriate poison, physicians were there to assist in this deliberate process, warranted by the belief in personal autonomy and freedom of choice versus the belief in God's ownership of human life, which dictates the way it is dealt with according to commandments imparted by so-called divine and authoritative scriptures. Their role was not, however, to provide like assistance to people who were merely depressed because of a coping problem in times of hardship. In that case, the pursuit of wisdom was advised, if normal cognitive abilities made it attainable. As for the famed Hippocratic oath, to promote health and abstain from causing harm, it included a discretionary option based on the physician's assessment of a given situation.

Christianity changed all that by the 12th century on religious grounds. It unconditionally condemns euthanasia as a violation of God's divine will, which allegedly upholds the absolute sanctity of life against any form of killing, including euthanasia or any form of suicide for that matter. Yet, life is not an absolute, and neither should the rules that apply to it. The right of self-defense in special instances of violent and potentially lethal aggression is an exemplary accommodation that sets an important precedent.

As regards the Christian church, however, it offers this sole and rather blurry compromise: a distinction between ordinary or proportionate and extraordinary or disproportionate means of care that are considered mandatory or not, respectively. It is gauged in terms of cost/benefit ratio that compares the amount of effort and distress to the relative merit of a therapy in improving someone's health.

In the 18th century, with the Age of Enlightenment, the Church's authority was challenged and the debate around euthanasia, reopened. Case in point, as the discovery of analgesics like morphine and chloroform was changing medicine, Samuel Williams (a non-physician) was advocating the use of these drugs for incurable and intolerable conditions, with the aim of alleviating this unnecessary torment and, more contentiously, expediting a patient's death. Allowing to die and causing death are two variations on the same theme that prompt all manner of hair-splitting nuances and mind-bending dilemmas. Having said that, can anyone claim with conviction that a gravely debilitated and benumbed existence, perfused with opiates, is one that can be viewed as good and worth sustaining?

Let's just say that until today the champions of euthanasia have been persistent and their movement is slowly gaining traction with the public, enough to influence policy, notwithstanding pockets of resistance among physicians, lawyers, politicians, social scientists, religious figures, and philosophers. This is all the more welcome as modern medicine has rendered possible the extension of life, absent the experience of well-being, sometimes for months, if not years, until death. This artificial extension is a socially created problem that calls for a social solution. After all, it appears safe to say that it is not the duration of life but its quality that matters most.

While there is a solid argument in favor of euthanasia, concerning unbearable and insuperable misery, any society that undertakes to legalize it within these bounds must also be mindful of the excesses that can follow as the prerequisites for euthanasia are gradually loosened.

The Netherlands, where euthanasia is practiced widely, is confronted with such an unwelcome development. Numerous assisted deaths that are reported annually are questionable at best if not downright scandalous. Consider the example of a divorced wife who was also a grieving mother, having lost her two sons; she was disconsolate and granted assistance by a psychiatrist to end her life. This example should make us pause and reflect.

Another valuable occasion to ponder euthanasia critically is the encyclical letter by Pope John Paul II, entitled *Evangelium Vitae* (1995). There, the Christian perspective is clearly expounded. According to his holiness, euthanasia goes against the will of God (as portrayed in the Bible and biblical exegeses) and the natural law. Again, as it is invariably done in the secular world, the authority of the holy book and other sacred texts can be disputed, which is a way of numbering these documents among other human narratives and expositions open to debate. What about the natural law? Is euthanasia truly in contradiction with it?

A good place to start our inquiry is once more ancient Greece, particularly the pre-Socratic philosopher Empedocles. The latter speaks of two divine and antagonistic principles: Love—a force of attraction—and Strife—a force of repulsion. Together they drive the perpetual cycle of creation and destruction that underpins order and disorder in the universe. Some 2600 years ago, this dualistic outlook amazingly foreshadowed the current view of modern physics pertaining to thermodynamics. In this view, entropy and negative entropy (negentropy for short) are the two magnetic poles that pull the evolutionary arrow, like the needle of a compass, toward an increase of structural and functional complexity, and ultimately toward life, or the reverse: chaos and death.

A notable and illustrative phenomenon to help us picture negentropy—thanks to which things become more orderly and lively, and presage the advent of life—is the dissipative structure or more specifically the eponymous Bénard cell from the French physicist Henri Bénard.

His claim to fame was the study of thermal convection in viscous fluids where the convective motions spontaneously formed cellular patterns with great dissipative properties. Whereas closed systems are isolated from their environment and hence free to reach their entropic end (i.e., a state of thermal equilibrium and disordered inertia), these fluids were open systems that remained dynamically ordered, far from thermal equilibrium, because of their exposure to a source of intense heat situated directly below. The molecules of the fluids closest to this source uniformly scattered, which reduced their density and weight relative to the molecules above and produced a convective upward flow due to buoyancy.

A troubling question springs to mind: If life can be regarded as a sophisticated form of dissipative structure, entailing an input and output of energy obtained from the environment, does it fall under the same implacable and dreadful logic as its homolog? The dissipative structure is a conditional and transitional occurrence designed to completely dissipate an unstabilizing inflow of heat and effectuate thermal equilibrium (in tandem with disordered inertia as a distinct symptom of entropy), provided the initial source of heat disappears. Ergo, does the big picture reveal this forbidding fact: The ultimate purpose of negentropy, order, and life is entropy, disorder, and death? Such a fact would lend credence to Freud's provocative contention (in *Beyond the Pleasure Principle*) according to which "The most universal endeavor of all living substance [is] to return to the quiescence of the inorganic world." Freud also talks of a "Nirvana principle," pointing to a tendency of organisms to resolve all tensions and bring them to zero, or what the Stoics from antiquity called ataraxy.

However, the Freudian "death instinct" might be a conceptual overkill. Although life shares with the dissipative structure the same basic mode of being as a dynamic entity organized from within but fueled from without, it adds to that foundation another layer of determination. Some 3.5 billion years ago, life presumably arose from the adoption of this basic mode of being as an ad hoc solution to the problem of instability in an antagonistic environment, which disrupted the equilibrium of its humble nonliving origin; but also, it committed this solution to genetic memory and thus guaranteed its reproduction indefinitely on condition that the environment remained conducive to viability.

Furthermore, unlike the rest of the animal kingdom that is exclusively or predominantly driven by instincts, genetically hardwired in the brain and proportionately rigid, with little to no margin of creative freedom, humans have the benefit of brain plasticity, which implies the ability to learn; they largely conform to a set of acquired habits that can be modified at will, in response to a change of circumstances or for the sake of variety. As a result, they are exceptionally adaptable or capable of turning an unfavorable situation around.

To put it otherwise, life infuses its nature as a dissipative structure with a new purpose, which makes its survival—through genetic mechanisms and strategic instincts or habits, necessary for the preservation of life—a goal in itself. And yet, this survival is doomed to expire eventually, both from the viewpoint of the individual and from that of the species to which this individual belongs. In sum, life only postpones the inevitable. Meanwhile, however, it proclaims its attachment to the business of living and repels death, in cahoots with the second law of thermodynamics. This law asserts the tendency of everything as a whole toward entropy, assuming that the universe is a closed system. But who knows? Perhaps this assumption should be punctuated with a question mark like all things human open to doubt.

Upon further review, one caveat stands out like a sore thumb: Life's attachment to the business of living depends on its relative success or failure in generating health and happiness. The more we experience sickness and suffering, the more this attachment changes to detachment, and far from relishing the perspective of future days, we revel in the prospect of an early exit. So it seems fair to suggest that the expression "death wish" is more consistent with our human psyche than the Freudian alternative, "death instinct." Contrary to the latter, the former is conditional and relates to extremely negative values of clearly identified variables: health and happiness. These values help us conceive of a critical threshold beyond which our love of life degenerates into the love of death.

We can therefore conclude that, psychologically, euthanasia is a perfectly understandable choice in dire circumstances that offer no hope a recovery. But does euthanasia also make sense from a biological point of view? The process of cellular suicide called "apoptosis" supports a positive, albeit tentative answer. To be precise, apoptosis serves the vital purpose of the organism by causing cells to precipitate their own destruction—under the control of particular genes and by means of specific enzymes—when their continued growth would prove burdensome or harmful to this organism because of total superfluity or excessive morbidity.

Could we regard as a logical extension of this biological process the deliberate termination of our multicellular existence—through the requested agency of a medical assistant in possession of a select poison—if persisting through dire circumstances that offer no hope of recovery would be truly unbearable and arguably pointless? We can answer in the affirmative if we consider that life suitably resorts to a mere pruning of unwanted cells when the organism is still by and large capable of weathering a bout of adversity and flourishing, whereas an insufferable and irremediable state of physical decay is reminiscent of a potted flower that has become withered and lifeless, and leaves no other sensible option than to remove it from the pot and let it complete the last stage of its decline until it turns to dust.

Summary of Between Life and Death:

1. Euthanasia has a long history that begins in ancient Greece where it was common practice
2. Its intent was "a good death:" a peaceful and voluntary passing under controlled circumstances to end suffering, particularly during a terminal illness

1. Christianity changed all that by the 12th century on religious grounds by affirming the absolute sanctity of life
2. Yet life is not an absolute and neither should the rules that apply to it

1. In the 18th century—Age of Enlightenment—the authority of the church was challenged and the debate around euthanasia, reopened
2. It is not the duration of life but its quality that matters most

1. From a psychological standpoint euthanasia is a perfectly understandable choice in dire circumstances that offer no hope of recovery
2. From a biological standpoint the process of cellular suicide called "apoptosis" arguably supports euthanasia in the same circumstances

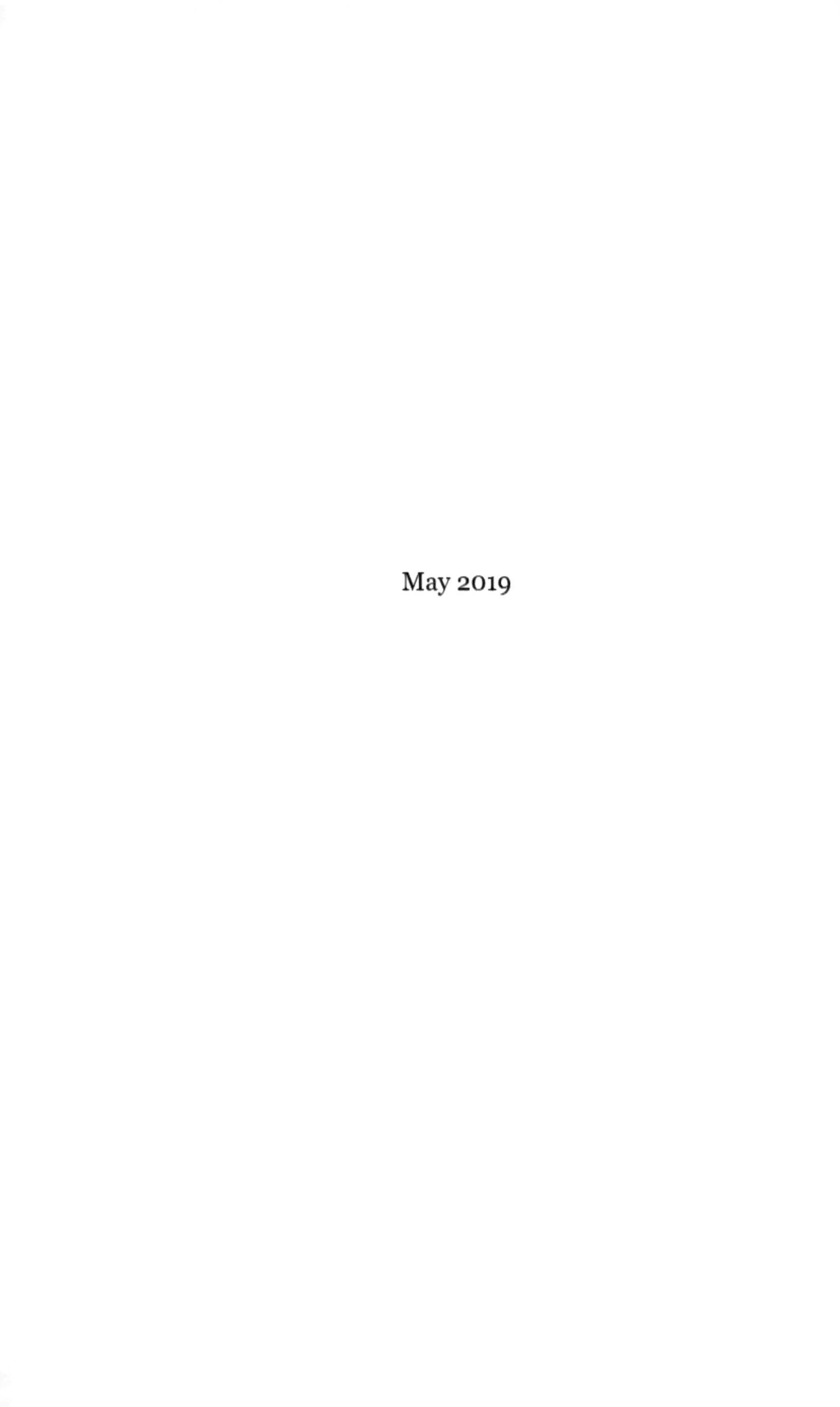

May 2019

www.ingramcontent.com/pod-product-compliance
Lightning Source LLC
Chambersburg PA
CBHW022215050726
47590CB00002B/814